A Guide to Mastering Wealth and Success by Zohaib Hassan Khan

About the Author:

Zohaib Hassan Khan is a renowned expert in wealth creation and success habits. With years of experience in finance, entrepreneurship, and personal development, Zohaib shares valuable insights to help individuals achieve their financial goals and live a fulfilling life.

Table of Contents

"Embark on the journey of success not merely to accumulate wealth, but to craft a legacy of positive impact—a legacy that transcends fortune and resonates in the lives of others. Your habits shape not just your success, but the indelible mark you leave on the world."

Chapter 1: Introduction

<u>Understanding the Millionaire Mindset</u>

In this chapter, readers embark on a journey to comprehend the intricate workings of the millionaire mindset. Through real-life anecdotes, psychological studies, and expert insights, we dissect the thought patterns, beliefs, and attitudes that set millionaires apart. Practical exercises guide readers in self-reflection to identify and nurture the mindset essential for financial success.

Importance of Habits in Wealth Creation

Building on the mindset exploration, we delve into the fundamental role of habits in shaping financial destinies. Readers gain an understanding of how seemingly small, consistent actions compound over time to create substantial wealth. Practical habit-building strategies are introduced, ensuring readers can implement these concepts into their daily lives.

Mastering the Psychology of Wealth

In the opening chapter, readers embark on a profound exploration of the psychological underpinnings that distinguish millionaires from the rest. This chapter serves as a gateway into the intricate workings of the millionaire mindset, unraveling the mental attitudes, beliefs, and thought patterns that contribute to financial success.

Key Components:

Understanding the Wealth Mindset: Delve into the core beliefs that underpin the mindset of successful individuals who have achieved financial prosperity. Uncover the ways in which they perceive opportunities, challenges, and their own capabilities.

Shaping Positive Financial Attitudes: Explore how positive attitudes toward money, risk, and abundance contribute to the foundation of wealth creation. Understand the importance of cultivating a mindset that attracts financial success rather than repelling it.

Overcoming Limiting Beliefs: Address common limiting beliefs that hinder financial progress. Provide practical strategies for identifying and overcoming self-imposed mental barriers, empowering readers to adopt a more expansive and optimistic mindset.

Visualization Techniques: Introduce visualization as a powerful tool for manifesting financial goals. Guide readers through exercises that help them vividly envision their desired financial future, fostering a sense of clarity and motivation.

Building Confidence in Financial Decision-Making: Discuss the role of confidence in making sound financial decisions. Provide insights into how a confident mindset influences risk-taking, investment choices, and overall financial success.

Practical Applications:

Self-Reflection Exercises: Engage readers in introspective exercises designed to help them assess their current beliefs and attitudes toward wealth. By identifying areas for growth, readers can actively work on aligning their mindset with financial success.

Real-Life Case Studies: Share real-life examples of individuals who transformed their mindset and, consequently, their financial circumstances. These case studies serve as inspiration and practical illustrations of the principles discussed.

Reader Takeaways:

Upon completing this chapter, readers will gain a comprehensive understanding of the mindset that underlies financial success. Armed with insights into the psychological principles at play, readers will be better equipped to align their thinking with the habits and behaviors necessary for their own wealth-building journey. This foundational knowledge sets the stage for the practical strategies and habits detailed in subsequent chapters.

Mastering the Psychology of Wealth in the Modern Era

In the context of the modern era, where technological advancements, changing economic landscapes, and shifting societal norms shape our daily lives, the exploration of the millionaire mindset takes on new relevance and applications.

Technological Mindset Integration:

Understanding the Digital Frontier: Explore how the modern millionaire mindset integrates technology. Discuss the role of digital tools, automation, and the online landscape in wealth creation. Illustrate how successful individuals leverage technology for financial gain and business innovation.

Adaptability to Change: Emphasize the need for adaptability in a rapidly evolving technological landscape. Successful individuals in the modern era often embrace change, leveraging new technologies and platforms to stay ahead in their financial endeavors.

Global Connectivity and Abundance Mentality:

Access to Global Opportunities: Discuss how the modern millionaire mindset transcends geographical boundaries. In an interconnected world, individuals can tap into global opportunities, fostering an abundance mentality that goes beyond traditional, localized thinking.

Impact of Information Overload: Acknowledge the challenges of navigating vast amounts of information. Guide readers on how to sift through the noise, stay informed, and cultivate a discerning mindset in the face of constant digital information.

Overcoming Limiting Beliefs in the Digital Age:

Digital Entrepreneurship as a Solution: Address common limiting beliefs associated with the digital realm, such as the fear of failure in online ventures. Showcase examples of digital entrepreneurs who overcame obstacles and transformed their mindset to achieve success.

Online Learning and Skill Development: Highlight the accessibility of online education and skill development platforms. Encourage readers to overcome limiting beliefs about acquiring new skills, leveraging the internet as a powerful resource for personal and professional growth.

Visualizing Digital Success:

Utilizing Visualization Apps and Tools: Introduce modern tools and applications that facilitate visualization exercises. From vision board apps to virtual reality experiences, provide readers with contemporary means to vividly picture their financial goals.

Social Media Influence: Discuss the impact of social media on shaping financial aspirations. Explore how curated online content and success stories shared on digital platforms contribute to the visualization process, fostering inspiration and motivation.

Confidence Building in a Connected World:

Online Communities and Support Networks: Explore the role of online communities in building confidence. From financial forums to social media groups, highlight how individuals can connect with like-minded peers, share experiences, and bolster their confidence in financial decision-making.

Digital Presence and Personal Branding: Discuss the importance of a strong digital presence in building confidence. Explore how individuals can strategically showcase their skills, achievements, and expertise online, contributing to a confident and influential online persona.

Practical Applications for the Digital Age:

Digital Mindset Assessment Tools: Integrate online tools and quizzes that help readers assess their digital mindset. These tools can provide personalized insights and recommendations for aligning their mindset with the demands of the digital era.

Interactive Webinars and Virtual Events: Extend the learning experience through interactive webinars or virtual events. Invite successful individuals from the digital space to share their experiences and engage with readers in real-time discussions.

Reader Takeaways for the Modern Era:

In navigating the complexities of the modern era, readers will gain not only a foundational understanding of the millionaire mindset but also practical insights into how this mindset is adapted and applied in the digital age. The chapter empowers readers to harness the opportunities presented by technology, overcome digital-age challenges, and cultivate a mindset that is not only resilient but thriving in the fast-paced, interconnected world of today.

Chapter 2: Blueprinting Success

Setting SMART Goals and Crafting a Wealth Plan

In the second chapter, readers embark on a strategic journey of goal setting and wealth planning. This chapter serves as a compass, guiding individuals to articulate clear, actionable goals and develop a comprehensive wealth plan to navigate the financial landscape effectively.

Key Components:

Understanding SMART Goals:

Specific: Guide readers on how to make their goals specific and clearly defined. For example, instead of a vague goal like "save money," encourage a specific target such as "save $10,000 for an emergency fund within the next 12 months."

Measurable: Emphasize the importance of quantifiable metrics to track progress. Discuss the role of measurable criteria in gauging success and adjusting strategies accordingly.

Achievable: Help readers set realistic goals aligned with their current circumstances and resources. Explore how setting achievable goals builds confidence and motivation.

Relevant: Discuss the significance of aligning goals with broader life aspirations. Encourage readers to evaluate the relevance of each goal to their overall vision for financial success.

Time-Bound: Illustrate the power of setting deadlines for each goal. Discuss how time-bound objectives create a sense of urgency and focus, driving individuals to take consistent action.

Crafting a Comprehensive Wealth Plan:

Budgeting Strategies: Dive into the intricacies of effective budgeting. Provide practical tools and templates for readers to create a budget tailored to their income, expenses, and financial goals.

Savings Goals: Discuss the importance of allocating a portion of income to savings. Guide readers in defining short-term and long-term savings goals, considering factors like emergencies, investments, and major purchases.

Investment Plans: Explore various investment options and strategies based on individual risk tolerance and financial objectives. Discuss the importance of diversification and long-term planning in building wealth.

Debt Management: Address the role of debt in financial planning. Provide actionable steps for managing and reducing debt strategically, minimizing its impact on long-term financial goals.

Practical Applications:

Goal-Setting Workshop:

Interactive Session: Conduct an interactive goal-setting workshop, either in-person or virtually. Guide participants through the process of articulating SMART goals, encouraging peer discussion and feedback.

Personal Goal Worksheets: Provide worksheets or online tools that readers can use to draft their goals. Include prompts to ensure each goal meets the SMART criteria.

Wealth Planning Toolkit:

Online Calculators: Share online calculators that assist in budgeting, savings projections, and investment planning. These tools can help readers visualize the potential outcomes of their financial decisions.

Checklists and Guides: Offer downloadable checklists and step-by-step guides for crafting a comprehensive wealth plan. Break down the process into manageable tasks, allowing readers to follow a structured approach.

Reader Action Steps:

Define SMART Goals:

Action: Spend dedicated time reflecting on personal and financial aspirations.

Task: Draft specific, measurable, achievable, relevant, and time-bound goals.

Craft a Wealth Plan:

Action: Evaluate current financial standing and future aspirations.

Task: Create a budget, set savings goals, outline an investment strategy, and develop a plan for debt management.

Regular Review and Adjustment:

Action: Establish a routine for reviewing financial goals and progress.

Task: Schedule quarterly or semi-annual reviews to assess achievements, adjust goals as needed, and refine the wealth plan.

Key Takeaways:

By the end of this chapter, readers will have not only a clear understanding of SMART goal setting and wealth planning but also tangible, personalized goals and a comprehensive plan for financial success. The emphasis on actionable steps and practical tools ensures that readers are equipped to turn their aspirations into a strategic roadmap for wealth creation.

Understanding SMART Goals:

Motivation Boost: Begin with stories of individuals who transformed their lives through goal setting. Share anecdotes of successful entrepreneurs, emphasizing the role of clear, specific, and time-bound goals in their journeys.

Visualization Exercise: Encourage readers to visualize their future success. Guide them through a reflective exercise where they vividly picture themselves achieving their most ambitious financial goals. This creates an emotional connection to their aspirations.

Setting a Personal Mantra: Motivate readers to create a personal mantra or affirmation tied to their financial goals. This could serve as a daily reminder of their objectives, fostering a positive mindset.

Crafting a Comprehensive Wealth Plan:

Inspiration from Financial Role Models: Share stories of renowned figures who meticulously planned their wealth journeys. Highlight the strategic financial planning methods of successful individuals, showcasing the impact of a well-crafted wealth plan.

Goal Breakdown Workshop: Conduct a workshop where readers break down their long-term financial goals into smaller, actionable steps. This provides a roadmap, making monumental aspirations feel more achievable.

Celebrate Milestones: Emphasize the importance of celebrating small victories along the way. Encourage readers to acknowledge and reward themselves when they achieve a milestone, reinforcing a positive connection to their financial journey.

Motivational Tools:

Visual Goal Board:

Create a Vision Board: Suggest the creation of a visual goal board. Encourage readers to cut out images, quotes, and symbols that represent their financial goals. Displaying this board prominently serves as a daily reminder of their aspirations.

Digital Goal Tracker: Recommend digital goal-tracking apps that visually represent progress. Seeing incremental successes boosts motivation and reinforces the belief that larger goals are within reach.

Wealth Manifesto:

Write a Wealth Manifesto: Inspire readers to articulate a personal wealth manifesto. This is a powerful written declaration of their financial goals, values, and commitment. Revisit and revise it regularly to stay aligned with their aspirations.

Share Manifestos: Encourage readers to share their wealth manifestos within a trusted community or online platform. This fosters accountability and creates a supportive network for mutual encouragement.

Reader Action Steps:

Create an Inspiring Space:

Action: Set aside dedicated time for creating a motivational space.

Task: Decorate a corner with inspiring quotes, images, and their vision board.

Daily Affirmations:

Action: Start each day with a positive affirmation.

Task: Craft a concise, powerful mantra related to their financial goals and repeat it daily.

Monthly Reflections:

Action: Establish a monthly reflection ritual.

Task: Reflect on achievements, celebrate milestones, and adjust goals if necessary.

Community Engagement:

Action: Connect with a like-minded community.

Task: Share goals and progress, providing and receiving motivation within the community.

Chapter 3: Financial Wisdom Unleashed

Continuous Learning and Smart Investment Strategies

As we delve into the mysteries of financial wisdom, this chapter invites readers into the uncharted territories of continuous learning and innovative investment strategies. Beyond conventional wisdom, this journey promises not only to enlighten but to empower, providing a deeper understanding of the ever-evolving landscape of financial success.

Beyond the Horizon:

Unveiling Hidden Market Trends:

Market Psychology Exploration: Venture into the intricate psychology of financial markets. Explore how market sentiments, investor behavior, and psychological biases shape

the ebb and flow of financial landscapes. Uncover the hidden cues that savvy investors use to navigate market trends.

Behavioral Economics Insights: Dive into the world of behavioral economics, revealing the psychological factors influencing financial decisions. Understand how cognitive biases impact investment choices and how awareness of these biases can be leveraged for financial gain.

Crypt currency Chronicles:

Decoding the Crypt currency Enigma: Embark on a captivating exploration of the mysterious world of crypto currencies. Uncover the origins, principles, and potential future impact of digital currencies. Navigate through the complexities of block chain technology and its transformative role in financial transactions.

Risk and Reward in the Crypto Realm: Delve into the risks and rewards associated with crypto currency investments. Navigate the volatile seas of digital assets, discovering strategies to capitalize on opportunities while safeguarding against potential pitfalls.

Suspenseful Revelations:

Insider Secrets of Investment Gurus:

Exclusive Interviews: Prepare for exclusive interviews with renowned investment gurus. Gain insights into their personal philosophies, strategies, and the untold stories behind their most significant financial triumphs. Unearth the wisdom that has propelled these individuals to the pinnacle of investment success.

Contrarian Investment Strategies: Challenge traditional investment norms with contrarian strategies. Explore the mindset of investors who thrive on going against the crowd. Learn how embracing contrarian views can uncover unique opportunities and lead to exceptional returns.

The Quantum Leap of Artificial Intelligence:

AI in Financial Forecasting: Step into the realm of artificial intelligence and its impact on financial forecasting. Discover how machine learning algorithms analyze vast datasets to predict market trends. Unravel the potential of AI in making informed investment decisions and staying ahead in a data-driven world.

Robot-Advisors Unveiled: Lift the veil on robot-advisors, AI-driven financial advisors that are revolutionizing investment management. Explore how these digital platforms provide personalized investment strategies, optimize portfolios, and democratize access to sophisticated financial advice.

Practical Secrets for Financial Alchemy:

Mastering Financial Alchemy:

Leveraging Financial Technology (Fitch): Explore the alchemy of Fitch, where technology meets finance. Uncover how Fitch innovations are reshaping banking, payments, and investment services. Learn to harness the power of financial technology to streamline financial operations and enhance wealth creation.

Algorithmic Trading Strategies: Peer into the realm of algorithmic trading, where complex algorithms execute trades with unprecedented speed and precision. Understand how algorithmic strategies are employed by institutional investors and discover ways to adapt these principles for individual wealth growth.

Actionable Steps for Financial Sorcery:

The Ritual of Lifelong Learning:

Book of Wisdom: Create a personalized "Book of Wisdom" to document insights from financial books, courses, and mentors. Regularly revisit this book as a sacred text guiding your financial journey.

Interactive Learning Rituals: Develop interactive learning rituals, incorporating podcasts, webinars, and online courses into your routine. Engage in financial discussions with peers, expanding your knowledge through shared insights.

Crypt currency Quest:

Crypto Challenge: Embark on a crypto challenge, allocating a portion of your investment portfolio to digital assets. Track the performance and learn from the experience, demystifying the world of crypto currencies through hands-on exploration.

Block chain Immersion: Immerse yourself in the world of block chain by actively participating in block chain communities. Contribute to projects, attend conferences, and embrace the decentralized ethos driving this technological revolution.

AI Empowerment Rituals:

AI-Assisted Portfolio Experiment: Experiment with AI-assisted portfolio management. Explore robot-advisors or algorithmic trading platforms to experience the power of artificial intelligence in optimizing your investment decisions.

Fitch Integration: Embrace Fitch solutions to streamline your financial processes. Explore budgeting apps, investment platforms, and digital banking services that leverage technology for financial efficiency.

The exploration of financial wisdom, encompassing continuous learning and smart investment strategies, holds paramount importance in the modern era for several compelling reasons:

Dynamic Financial Landscape:

The financial landscape is in a perpetual state of evolution. Global markets, technological advancements, and regulatory changes constantly reshape the economic terrain. Continuous learning is essential to navigate these shifts and make informed decisions in an ever-changing environment.

Wealth Creation and Preservation:

The pursuit of financial wisdom is intricately linked to wealth creation and preservation. Smart investment strategies, grounded in a deep understanding of market trends and innovative approaches, empower individuals to not only grow their wealth but also safeguard it against potential risks.

Technological Disruption:

The rise of financial technology (Fitch), crypto currencies, and artificial intelligence has disrupted traditional financial paradigms. Understanding these technological advancements is crucial for individuals seeking to leverage these tools for efficient financial management and investment.

Empowerment through Knowledge:

Knowledge is a powerful tool for empowerment. In the realm of finance, being well-informed allows individuals to take control of their financial destiny. Continuous learning provides the insights and tools needed to make strategic decisions, reducing reliance on external advice.

Mitigating Risks and Maximizing Returns:

Unveiling hidden market trends, exploring crypto currency opportunities, and leveraging artificial intelligence in financial decisions are not just theoretical pursuits. These actions are tangible strategies to mitigate risks and maximize returns, ensuring that financial goals are not merely aspirations but achievable milestones.

Adaptability in a Fast-Paced World:

The ability to adapt to change is a hallmark of success. Continuous learning equips individuals with the flexibility and adaptability required to thrive in a fast-paced, dynamic world. This is particularly relevant in the financial realm, where the ability to adapt to new technologies and market trends is paramount.

Building Resilience against Uncertainty:

Financial uncertainty is a constant in life. By understanding the intricacies of financial markets, investment strategies, and technological trends, individuals build resilience against economic uncertainties. This resilience allows for a more secure financial future, even in the face of unexpected challenges.

Democratization of Financial Knowledge:

The democratization of financial knowledge is a recent phenomenon, facilitated by the accessibility of information through digital platforms. Individuals can now empower themselves with financial wisdom, irrespective of their background or traditional access to financial education.

Entrepreneurial Ventures:

For aspiring entrepreneurs, understanding financial principles is a non-negotiable aspect of success. Whether launching a startup or navigating the complexities of business finance, the insights gained from continuous learning form the bedrock of entrepreneurial ventures.

Strategic Decision-Making for Financial Independence:

Ultimately, the pursuit of financial wisdom is a pathway to financial independence. By making strategic decisions based on a deep understanding of financial principles, individuals can shape their financial destinies, breaking free from financial constraints and achieving true independence.

In summary, the importance of exploring financial wisdom lies in its transformative potential. It is not merely a theoretical pursuit but a practical and empowering journey toward financial security, growth, and independence in an ever-evolving world.

Chapter 4: Time Mastery for Prosperity

Maximizing Productivity and Strategic Task Prioritization

In the unfolding narrative of financial success, Chapter 4 serves as a compass through the intricacies of time mastery. The ability to harness time efficiently is not just a skill; it is a cornerstone for prosperity. This chapter illuminates the art of productivity, strategic task prioritization, and the profound impact these elements can have on one's journey toward financial abundance.

The Essence of Time Mastery:

Productivity Paradigms Unveiled:

Deep Work Principles: Dive into the philosophy of deep work, where focused, uninterrupted periods of concentration lead to heightened productivity. Explore strategies to cultivate deep work habits and carve out undistracted time for tasks that move the needle.

Time Blocking Strategies: Uncover the power of time blocking, a technique where specific blocks of time are allocated to distinct tasks. Learn how this method enhances efficiency, reduces multitasking, and contributes to a more organized and productive day.

Strategic Task Prioritization:

Eisenhower Matrix Mastery: Introduce the Eisenhower Matrix, a powerful tool for task prioritization. Delve into the distinction between urgent and important tasks and guide readers in categorizing and addressing responsibilities with strategic precision.

The 2-Minute Rule: Explore the simplicity of the 2-minute rule, where tasks that take two minutes or less are tackled immediately. Understand how this rule minimizes procrastination and contributes to a sense of accomplishment throughout the day.

Time as a Wealth-Building Asset:

Investing Time in High-Value Activities:

Opportunity Cost Awareness: Instill a heightened awareness of opportunity costs. Illustrate how every moment invested in one activity is a choice that carries implications for potential gains or losses elsewhere. Empower readers to make conscious choices aligned with their financial goals.

Compound Effect in Time Management: Draw parallels between time management and the compound effect in finance. Showcase how consistent, strategic time investments in high-value activities lead to compounded returns over the long term.

Building Sustainable Habits:

Habit Stacking Techniques: Introduce the concept of habit stacking, where new behaviors are integrated into existing routines. Guide readers in incorporating productive habits seamlessly into their daily lives, fostering a sustainable approach to time mastery.

Rituals for Peak Productivity: Explore rituals that precede high-productivity sessions. Whether its morning routines, mindfulness practices, or pre-task rituals, these activities set the stage for peak performance and sustained focus.

Practical Applications and Tactical Strategies:

Time Audit Workshop:

Personal Time Audit: Conduct a workshop guiding readers through a personal time audit. Encourage them to track activities throughout the day, identifying patterns and areas for improvement. Provide tools to analyze and optimize time allocation.

Goal-Alignment Session: Facilitate a session where readers align their daily activities with their overarching financial goals. This exercise fosters a connection between daily actions and long-term aspirations.

Strategic Prioritization Toolkit:

Eisenhower Matrix Templates: Provide templates for Eisenhower Matrix prioritization. Readers can use these tools to categorize tasks based on urgency and importance, creating a visual guide for strategic decision-making.

Task Prioritization Challenge: Challenge readers to a task prioritization challenge. Encourage them to apply the 2-minute rule, time blocking, and the Eisenhower Matrix for a set period, gauging the impact on productivity and overall sense of control.

Reader Action Steps for Time Prosperity:

Deep Work Commitment:

Action: Dedicate specific time slots for deep work.

Task: Identify tasks that require focused attention and allocate dedicated time for deep, uninterrupted work.

Eisenhower Matrix Mastery:

Action: Implement the Eisenhower Matrix for task prioritization.

Task: Categorize pending tasks into urgent-important, important-not urgent, urgent-not important, and neither urgent nor important.

Time Blocking Experiment:

Action: Experiment with time blocking for increased productivity.

Task: Allocate specific blocks of time to different categories of tasks, ensuring a balance between work, personal development, and leisure.

Habit Stacking Ritual:

Action: Establish habit stacking rituals for consistent productivity.

Task: Identify an existing habit and stack a new, productive habit onto it, creating a seamless integration into daily routines.

Time and finance share a profound and direct relationship that significantly influences an individual's financial well-being. Understanding this interconnection is crucial for making informed decisions and optimizing wealth creation. Here are key aspects of the direct relationship between time and finance:

Compound Interest:

The Power of Compounding: Time is a critical factor in the power of compounding, one of the most potent principles in finance. The longer money is invested, the more time it has to generate returns, and these returns, in turn, contribute to a growing base for future earnings. Time magnifies the impact of compound interest, making early investments more valuable.

Effect on Investments: Given enough time, even relatively modest investments can grow substantially. This emphasizes the importance of starting to invest early in life, allowing the compounding effect to work over an extended period.

Long-Term Investment Horizon:

Patience and Market Volatility: Time provides a buffer against market volatility. For long-term investors, the short-term fluctuations in the market become less significant. With a longer time horizon, individuals can weather market ups and downs, staying focused on their financial goals.

Retirement Planning: The direct relationship between time and finance is evident in retirement planning. Starting to save and invest for retirement early in one's career allows for more time to accumulate wealth, reducing the financial burden and providing a more comfortable retirement.

Opportunity Cost:

The Cost of Delay: Time plays a crucial role in the concept of opportunity cost. Delaying financial decisions, such as saving for goals or investing, can result in missed opportunities for wealth accumulation. The longer one delays, the greater the potential opportunity cost.

Leveraging Time for Investments: Individuals who harness the power of time make deliberate choices that align with their financial goals. Whether it's investing in education, career development, or entrepreneurial ventures, these choices leverage time as a valuable resource.

Career Progression and Earning Potential:

Career Growth over Time: Over a career, individuals often experience salary increases, promotions, and skill development. Time in the workforce can enhance earning potential, contributing to a higher income that, if managed wisely, can be directed toward financial goals.

Investing in Skills and Education: Investing time in acquiring new skills and education can enhance career prospects and open doors to higher-paying opportunities. This, in turn, has a direct impact on financial growth over the long term.

Debt Management and Time:

Time as a Debt Repayment Ally: Time can be a friend or foe when it comes to debt. Managing and reducing debt over time is essential for financial health. Individuals who strategically allocate time to pay down debts, especially high-interest ones, position themselves for greater financial freedom.

Avoiding Procrastination: Delaying debt repayment can result in additional interest and financial strain. Time, when used wisely, allows for systematic debt reduction, freeing up resources for other financial goals.

In essence, the direct relationship between time and finance underscores the importance of strategic planning, early action, and a long-term perspective. By recognizing the impact of time on various financial elements, individuals can make informed decisions that align with their goals and aspirations. The financial journey becomes not just a snapshot of the present but a dynamic, evolving story shaped by the passage of time.

NOW HOW TO MANAGE THE TIME

Effective time management is a crucial skill that directly impacts your ability to achieve financial goals and maintain a balanced, fulfilling life. Here are practical strategies to manage your time effectively:

1. Set Clear Goals:

Financial Objectives: Clearly define your financial goals, whether it's saving for a home, investing for retirement, or paying off debt. Break these goals into smaller, actionable steps.

Life Balance: Consider personal goals and aspirations. A well-rounded approach to goal-setting ensures that you're not neglecting other essential aspects of life, such as health, relationships, and personal development.

2. Prioritize Tasks:

Eisenhower Matrix: Prioritize tasks using the Eisenhower Matrix, categorizing them into urgent/important, important/not urgent, urgent/not important, and neither urgent nor important. Focus on high-priority tasks to maximize productivity.

Time Blocking: Allocate specific blocks of time for different types of tasks. Designate periods for deep work, meetings, personal development, and leisure. This helps maintain focus and prevents tasks from overlapping.

3. Create a Schedule:

Daily and Weekly Planning: Start each day with a clear plan of tasks to tackle. Additionally, plan your week in advance, considering both work and personal commitments. A well-organized schedule fosters efficiency.

Use Technology: Leverage digital tools like calendars, task management apps, and reminders to stay organized. Set alerts for important deadlines and appointments.

4. Learn to Say No:

Prioritize Commitments: Assess the importance of new commitments against your existing priorities. Politely decline tasks or projects that don't align with your current goals or may overwhelm your schedule.

Establish Boundaries: Learn to set boundaries to protect your time. Communicate your availability and be assertive in managing demands on your schedule.

5. Avoid Multitasking:

Focus on Deep Work: Multitasking can decrease overall productivity. Instead, focus on deep work by concentrating on one task at a time. This enhances the quality of your work and reduces errors.

Batch Similar Tasks: Group similar tasks together to minimize context switching. For instance, handle all emails in one batch, make phone calls together, and dedicate a specific time for creative work.

6. Effective Delegation:

Delegate Appropriately: Recognize tasks that can be delegated without compromising quality. This could involve assigning responsibilities at work or sharing household tasks.

Outsource When Possible: Consider outsourcing tasks that don't require your specific expertise. This could include hiring professionals for certain financial or administrative responsibilities.

7. Time for Reflection and Learning:

Regular Reviews: Periodically review your goals and adjust your schedule accordingly. This ensures that your actions align with your evolving priorities.

Continuous Improvement: Invest time in learning and improving time management skills. Attend workshops, read books, or explore online resources to discover new techniques and strategies.

8. Maintain Work-Life Balance:

Set Boundaries: Establish clear boundaries between work and personal life. Avoid overworking, and make time for relaxation, hobbies, and spending quality time with loved ones.

Scheduled Breaks: Incorporate short breaks into your workday. This can enhance productivity by preventing burnout and maintaining mental clarity.

9. Adaptability and Flexibility:

Be Flexible: Life is dynamic, and unexpected events may occur. Build flexibility into your schedule to accommodate unforeseen circumstances without causing stress.

Learn to Pivot: If a particular strategy or routine is not working, be willing to pivot. Regularly assess the effectiveness of your time management approach and make adjustments as needed.

10. Mindfulness and Well-Being:

Practice Mindfulness: Incorporate mindfulness practices into your routine, such as meditation or deep breathing exercises. This fosters mental clarity and reduces stress.

Physical Well-Being: Prioritize your health by allocating time for regular exercise and maintaining a balanced diet. Physical well-being positively impacts your overall energy levels and productivity.

Effective time management is a continuous process of self-awareness, planning, and adaptation. By implementing these strategies, you can optimize your use of time, enhance productivity, and create a conducive environment for achieving your financial objectives while maintaining a balanced and fulfilling life.

Chapter 5: Financial Fitness: Building a Strong Monetary Foundation

Balancing Budgets, Debt Management, and Wealth Building Strategies

Chapter 5 propels readers into the realm of financial fitness—a crucial juncture where the practical aspects of budgeting, debt management, and wealth-building strategies converge. Strengthening your financial foundation is akin to fortifying the pillars that support your wealth journey. This chapter unfolds as a comprehensive guide, providing actionable steps to achieve fiscal health and resilience.

Budget Mastery for Financial Stability:

Creating a Realistic Budget:

Assessment of Income and Expenses: Conduct a thorough assessment of your income sources and regular expenses. Categorize expenditures into fixed and variable, distinguishing needs from wants.

Setting Financial Goals: Align your budget with short-term and long-term financial goals. Allocate funds to specific objectives such as debt repayment, emergency savings, and investments.

Expense Tracking Techniques:

Utilizing Budgeting Apps: Explore the multitude of budgeting apps available. Leverage technology to effortlessly track expenditures, set spending limits, and receive real-time insights into your financial habits.

Cash Flow Analysis: Perform regular cash flow analyses to understand how money moves in and out of your accounts. Identify patterns and make informed adjustments to optimize your financial flow.

Debt Management Strategies:

Debt Assessment and Prioritization:

Inventory of Debts: Compile a comprehensive list of all outstanding debts, including credit cards, loans, and other financial obligations. Organize them by interest rates and total balances.

Prioritizing High-Interest Debts: Adopt a strategic approach to debt repayment by prioritizing high-interest debts. Allocate additional funds to pay off these debts more rapidly, saving on interest in the long run.

Consolidation and Negotiation Techniques:

Debt Consolidation Exploration: Investigate the option of consolidating high-interest debts into a single, lower-interest loan. Evaluate the feasibility and potential cost savings associated with consolidation.

Negotiating with Creditors: Initiate conversations with creditors to negotiate lower interest rates or more favorable repayment terms. Many creditors are willing to work with individuals facing financial challenges.

Wealth-Building Strategies:

Emergency Fund Establishment:

Setting Savings Targets: Determine an appropriate emergency fund size based on your lifestyle and financial responsibilities. Aim to cover three to six months' worth of living expenses.

Automated Savings Practices: Implement automated transfers to your emergency fund. Consistent contributions, even if small, accumulate over time, forming a financial safety net.

Investment Initiatives for Long-Term Growth:

Introduction to Investment Vehicles: Delve into the world of investments, exploring options such as stocks, bonds, and mutual funds. Understand the risk and return profiles of different investment vehicles.

Diversification Principles: Embrace the principle of diversification by spreading investments across various asset classes. This mitigates risk and enhances the potential for long-term growth.

Retirement Planning and Pension Contributions:

Strategic Retirement Planning: Strategize for retirement by contributing regularly to retirement accounts such as 401(k) s or IRAs. Leverage employer-sponsored plans and take advantage of any matching contributions.

Assessment of Pension Options: If applicable, explore pension options and assess their impact on your overall retirement income. Seek professional advice to optimize your pension strategy.

Practical Implementation Strategies:

Financial Workshop:

Budgeting Boot camp: Conduct a budgeting workshop, guiding readers through the process of creating a personalized budget. Provide templates and tools to facilitate hands-on budget development.

Debt Repayment Challenge: Initiate a debt repayment challenge, encouraging readers to allocate a specific percentage of their income toward debt reduction each month. Track progress and celebrate milestones.

Wealth-Building Simulation:

Investment Simulation: Create an investment simulation, allowing readers to experiment with different investment scenarios. Illustrate the impact of consistent contributions and the power of compound growth.

Emergency Fund Game Plan: Facilitate a game plan session for building emergency funds. Encourage readers to set realistic savings targets and implement actionable steps to achieve them.

Reader Action Steps for Financial Fitness:

Budgeting Commitment:

Action: Create a detailed budget based on your current financial situation.

Task: Identify areas for potential savings and allocate funds toward financial goals.

Debt Repayment Strategy:

Action: Develop a debt repayment strategy.

Task: Prioritize high-interest debts, negotiate with creditors, and explore consolidation options.

Emergency Fund Initiation:

Action: Initiate the establishment of an emergency fund.

Task: Set a specific savings target, automate contributions, and create a timeline for achieving your emergency fund goal.

Introduction to Investments:

Action: Begin exploring investment options.

Task: Research different investment vehicles and consider consulting with a financial advisor to align investments with your financial goals.

Retirement Planning Commitment:

Action: Commit to strategic retirement planning.

Task: Assess current retirement accounts, maximize contributions, and explore additional retirement planning options.

Key Takeaways:

Chapter 5 serves as a cornerstone for readers to fortify their financial foundation. By mastering budgeting, effectively managing debt, and strategically building wealth, individuals embark on a transformative journey toward lasting financial fitness. The practical implementation strategies and reader action steps ensure that the principles outlined become actionable milestones on the path to financial resilience and prosperity

Focusing on building a strong financial foundation requires a combination of mindset, discipline, and strategic actions. Here are key steps to stay focused on creating a robust financial base:

1. Clarify Your Financial Goals:

Define Clear Objectives: Clearly articulate your short-term and long-term financial goals. Whether it's saving for an emergency fund, paying off debt, or investing for retirement, having well-defined objectives provides a roadmap for your financial journey.

Prioritize Goals: Establish a hierarchy among your financial goals. Prioritize them based on urgency, importance, and their alignment with your overall life objectives.

2. Create a Realistic Budget:

Detailed Expense Analysis: Develop a comprehensive budget that accurately reflects your income and expenses. Scrutinize spending patterns to identify areas where adjustments can be made.

Allocate Funds Strategically: Distribute your income intentionally, allocating funds toward essential expenses, debt repayment, savings, and investments. Ensure that your budget aligns with your financial goals.

3. Debt Repayment Strategy:

Prioritize High-Interest Debts: Focus on paying off high-interest debts first. Devote extra funds to accelerate the repayment of debts with the highest interest rates.

Consolidation and Negotiation: Explore debt consolidation options and negotiate with creditors to potentially secure more favorable terms. A consolidated approach can simplify payments and reduce overall interest.

4. Emergency Fund Establishment:

Set Clear Savings Targets: Define specific targets for your emergency fund. This fund serves as a financial safety net, providing security in times of unexpected expenses or income disruptions.

Automate Savings: Facilitate consistent contributions to your emergency fund by setting up automated transfers. This ensures that saving becomes a routine part of your financial habits.

5. Invest Strategically for Growth:

Educate Yourself: Learn about different investment options and strategies. Understand the risk-return profiles of investments and align them with your financial goals and risk tolerance.

Start Early and Stay Consistent: Begin investing as early as possible and maintain consistent contributions over time. The power of compound interest is maximized with a long-term and disciplined approach.

6. Retirement Planning Commitment:

Assess Retirement Accounts: Evaluate your existing retirement accounts and explore additional retirement planning options. Maximize contributions to employer-sponsored plans and individual retirement accounts (IRAs).

Diversify Retirement Investments: Diversify your retirement investments to spread risk and enhance long-term growth potential. Consider consulting with a financial advisor to optimize your retirement strategy.

7. Regular Financial Check-Ins:

Scheduled Reviews: Establish regular intervals for financial check-ins. periodically review your budget, debt repayment progress, and the performance of your investments. Adjust your strategies based on changing circumstances.

Celebrate Milestones: Acknowledge and celebrate financial milestones. Whether it's reaching a savings goal, paying off a significant portion of debt, or achieving investment returns, celebrate these achievements to stay motivated.

8. Continuous Learning and Adaptation:

Stay Informed: Keep abreast of financial trends, investment opportunities, and changes in the economic landscape. Continuous learning empowers you to make informed decisions.

Adapt to Changes: Be adaptable in your financial approach. Life circumstances, economic conditions, and personal goals may evolve. Adjust your strategies as needed to stay aligned with your objectives.

9. Seek Professional Guidance:

Financial Advisor Consultation: Consider consulting with a financial advisor. Professional advice can provide personalized insights, address specific financial challenges, and optimize your overall financial plan.

Educate Yourself: While seeking guidance, actively participate in the decision-making process. Educate yourself on financial matters to make informed choices and collaborate effectively with financial professionals.

10. Cultivate a Financially Healthy Mindset:

Positive Affirmations: Adopt a positive mindset toward your financial journey. Use affirmations to reinforce your commitment to building a strong foundation and achieving financial success.

Learn from Challenges: View financial challenges as opportunities for growth. Learn from setbacks, reassess strategies, and use each experience to enhance your financial acumen.

Building a strong financial foundation is a dynamic process that requires ongoing attention and commitment. By staying focused on your goals, consistently implementing sound financial practices, and adapting to changes, you can create a resilient financial base that supports your aspirations and contributes to long-term financial well-being.

Chapter 6: **THE ART OF STRATEGIC SAVING**

Unlocking the Power of Systematic Savings and Smart Financial Habits

Chapter 6 immerses readers in the art of strategic saving—a cornerstone of financial success. Strategic saving goes beyond mere accumulation; it involves intentional planning, disciplined habits, and the foresight to transform savings into impactful financial decisions. This chapter unveils the secrets to strategic saving, offering actionable steps to harness its transformative power.

Building a Saving Mindset:

Mindful Spending Habits:

Conscious Consumption: Cultivate a mindset of conscious consumption. Assess your spending habits, differentiating between needs and wants. Intentional spending paves the way for more substantial savings.

The Power of Delayed Gratification: Embrace delayed gratification as a guiding principle. Prioritize long-term financial goals over immediate impulses, fostering a disciplined approach to spending and saving.

Goal-Oriented Saving:

S.M.A.R.T. Goals: Set Specific, Measurable, Achievable, Relevant, and Time-bound (S.M.A.R.T.) saving goals. Whether it's for an emergency fund, a vacation, or a major purchase, clearly defined goals provide direction.

Automated Savings Plans: Implement automated transfers to savings accounts. Automation ensures consistent contributions to your savings goals, minimizing the risk of overspending.

Strategies for Strategic Saving:

Pay Yourself First:

Priority Savings Allocation: Prioritize saving by adopting the "pay yourself first" principle. Allocate a portion of your income to savings before addressing other expenses. This ensures that saving is a non-negotiable part of your financial routine.

Incremental Increases: Gradually increase the percentage of income directed toward savings. As your income grows, adjust your savings contributions to maintain a proportional and meaningful savings rate.

Emergency Fund Mastery:

Emergency Fund Adequacy: Assess the adequacy of your emergency fund. Ensure that it covers essential living expenses for three to six months. Adjust the fund size based on changes in income, expenses, and life circumstances.

Replenishment Strategies: Establish a plan for replenishing the emergency fund after withdrawals. Consistent efforts to restore the fund maintain its effectiveness as a financial safety net.

Strategic Saving in Practice:

Budgeting for Savings:

Savings as a Non-Negotiable Expense: Treat savings as a fixed expense in your budget. Allocate a specific percentage of your income to savings before addressing discretionary spending.

Review and Adjust:* Regularly review your budget to identify opportunities for increased savings. As your financial situation evolves, make adjustments to align your savings goals with changing circumstances.

Savings Bucket System:

Categorize Savings Goals: Adopt a savings bucket system by categorizing goals into short-term, medium-term, and long-term buckets. Allocate funds accordingly, ensuring that each goal has a dedicated savings pool.

Visualize Progress: Use visual aids, such as charts or diagrams, to track the progress of your savings buckets.

Visualization enhances motivation and provides a tangible representation of your financial achievements.

Reader Engagement and Implementation:

Savings Challenge:

30-Day Savings Challenge: Launch a 30-day savings challenge to engage readers actively. Encourage them to identify and eliminate discretionary expenses for a month, directing the saved funds toward a specific savings goal.

Reflection and Insights: At the end of the challenge, prompt readers to reflect on their spending habits and identify sustainable changes. This self-awareness contributes to long-term financial well-being.

Emergency Fund Simulation:

Emergency Fund Simulation Exercise: Conduct a simulation exercise to help readers understand the impact of different emergency fund sizes. Analyze hypothetical scenarios to underscore the importance of financial preparedness.

Interactive Session: Facilitate an interactive session where readers share their emergency fund strategies and collectively explore optimal approaches to emergency fund management.

Strategic Saving for Future Wealth:

Investing Savings for Growth:

Introduction to Investment Vehicles: Educate readers on the potential for wealth growth through strategic investment of savings. Explore different investment vehicles and their suitability for varying time horizons.

Risk Tolerance Assessment: Assist readers in assessing their risk tolerance to align investment strategies with their comfort level. Highlight the role of risk and return in making informed investment decisions.

Long-Term Wealth-Building Strategies:

Retirement Savings Blueprint: Guide readers in developing a blueprint for retirement savings. Emphasize the importance of starting early, maximizing employer-sponsored plans, and diversifying investments for long-term growth.

Wealth Preservation Principles: Introduce wealth preservation strategies for the long term. Cover topics such as estate planning, insurance, and ongoing financial education to safeguard accumulated wealth.

Leveraging Strategic Saving as a Financial Weapon

Chapter 6 not only emphasizes the importance of strategic saving but also underscores the transformative potential of using accumulated savings as a formidable financial weapon. The objective is not merely to hoard funds but to strategically deploy them for significant financial milestones and opportunities. Here's how readers can wield their savings as a powerful financial weapon:

**1. Strategic Deployment for Financial Goals:

Goal Fulfillment: Saving is not an end in itself; it is a means to achieve financial goals. Encourage readers to identify and prioritize their financial goals—whether it's buying a home, starting a business, or funding education.

Tactical Savings Allocation: Demonstrate the power of tactical savings allocation. As specific savings goals are achieved, guide readers in strategically deploying these funds to realize their aspirations.

**2. Investment for Wealth Multiplication:

Wealth-Building Opportunities: Shift the focus from traditional saving to wealth multiplication through strategic investments. Illustrate how wisely invested funds can grow significantly over time, surpassing the returns of conventional savings accounts.

Compound Interest Advantage: Emphasize the compound interest advantage associated with investments. Educate readers on the compounding effect that can exponentially increase wealth over the long term.

**3. Entrepreneurial Ventures and Investments:

Seed Capital for Ventures: Position savings as seed capital for entrepreneurial ventures. Inspire readers to explore business opportunities, using their savings as the initial investment to kick start their ventures.

Diversified Investment Portfolios: Encourage the creation of diversified investment portfolios. Whether its stocks, bonds, or real estate, showcase how a well-balanced portfolio can mitigate risks and optimize returns.

**4. Strategic Debt Management:

Debt Consolidation and Elimination: Introduce the concept of using savings strategically for debt consolidation or elimination. Illustrate how deploying savings to pay off high-interest debts can lead to significant financial savings in the long run.

Negotiating with Creditors: Guide readers in negotiating with creditors using their savings as leverage. Negotiations may result in reduced interest rates or more favorable terms, freeing up additional funds for strategic financial moves.

**5. Realizing Major Life Milestones:

Homeownership: Paint a vivid picture of how savings can be the key to homeownership. By accumulating a substantial down payment, individuals can secure favorable mortgage terms and embark on the journey of property ownership.

Education Funding: Position savings as a tool for funding education. Whether for personal development or children's education, show how strategic saving can pave the way for educational pursuits.

**6. Emergency Fund as a Shield and Springboard:

Financial Safety Net: Reinforce the concept of the emergency fund as a financial shield. Savings act as a safety net during unforeseen circumstances, preventing individuals from falling into financial distress.

Springboard for Opportunities: Highlight how a well-maintained emergency fund can serve as a springboard for seizing unexpected opportunities. Whether it's an investment opportunity or a career pivot, having savings provides the flexibility to take calculated risks.

***7. Philanthropy and Legacy Building:

Charitable Contributions: Encourage readers to consider using their savings for charitable contributions. Philanthropy not only contributes to the greater good but can also have potential tax benefits.

Legacy Planning: Introduce the concept of legacy planning. Strategic saving can play a crucial role in building a financial legacy that extends beyond one's lifetime, benefiting future generations.

***8. Continuous Financial Evolution:

Adaptability and Innovation: Emphasize the importance of adaptability and innovation in financial decisions. The financial landscape evolves, and readers should be prepared to adapt their strategies, utilizing savings as a versatile tool.

Continuous Learning: Instill a commitment to continuous financial learning. Encourage readers to stay informed about new investment opportunities, financial instruments, and strategies that can enhance the effectiveness of their financial weapon.

Chapter 6, therefore, positions strategic saving not as a passive act but as an active financial weapon. It arms readers with the knowledge and mindset to deploy their savings strategically, unlocking doors to wealth multiplication, goal fulfillment, entrepreneurial endeavors, and meaningful contributions to society. By mastering the art of deploying savings as a financial weapon, individuals embark on a journey where their financial prowess becomes a force for creating the future they envision.

Chapter 7: The Symphony of Financial Harmony

Unveiling the Melody of Balanced Budgets and Financial Wellness

In Chapter 7, we embark on a captivating journey through the symphony of financial harmony—a harmonious blend of budgeting virtuosity, investment crescendos, and the sweet serenade of wealth-building strategies. As readers delve into this chapter, they are invited to enjoy the rhythmic interplay of financial instruments, each contributing to the creation of a masterpiece: a balanced and fulfilling financial life.

**1. Budgeting Ballet: The Dance of Income and Expenses:

Choreographing Finances: Imagine your finances as a ballet, each expense and income source gracefully pirouetting across the stage. Delve into the art of budgeting, where the dance of financial elements is choreographed to achieve a harmonious balance.

Budgeting Techniques: Introduce readers to various budgeting techniques, from traditional approaches to modern digital tools. Let them choose the rhythm that resonates with their financial style.

The Crescendo of Savings: Elevate the budgeting performance to a crescendo by highlighting the role of savings. Just as a ballet builds to a climax, a well-crafted budget crescendos with strategic savings allocations.

**2. Investment Sonatas: Crafting Melodies of Wealth:

The Orchestra of Investments: Picture your investments as a grand orchestra, each instrument playing a vital role. Uncover the secrets of investment symphonies, exploring the

diversity of instruments such as stocks, bonds, and mutual
funds.

Conducting the Investment Orchestra: Guide readers in
conducting their investment orchestra with skill and
precision. Emphasize the importance of diversification,
where each investment instrument plays its part in creating a
harmonious financial melody.

The Overture of Compound Growth: Illuminate the overture
of compound growth, where the orchestra's harmony
magnifies over time. Help readers appreciate the beauty of
patient investing and the sweet rewards of compounding.

**3. Wealth-Building Waltz: A Dance of Financial Flourish:

The Graceful Waltz of Wealth Building: Envision wealth
building as an elegant waltz, a dance of financial flourish.
Explore long-term strategies that gracefully navigate
through the twists and turns of economic landscapes.

Strategic Choreography of Financial Goals: Choreograph
the waltz of financial goals, demonstrating how each step
contributes to the overall dance. Whether it's buying a home
or funding education, every move is a deliberate and
beautiful part of the wealth-building performance.

Celebrating Milestone Dances: Encourage readers to
celebrate their financial waltz milestones. Whether it's

achieving a savings goal or reaching a significant investment benchmark, these moments are like triumphant dance sequences in their financial journey.

**4. The Serenade of Financial Freedom:

Harmony in Financial Independence: Unveil the serenade of financial freedom, a soothing melody that accompanies the pursuit of financial independence. Explore concepts of passive income, smart debt management, and the liberation that comes with a sound financial plan.

Conducting the Symphony of Debt Freedom: Illustrate the symphony of debt freedom, where each payment is a note in the composition. Guide readers through the journey of strategically eliminating debt to create a harmonious financial future.

**5. The Crescendo of Financial Education:

Educational Crescendo: Imagine financial education as a crescendo, a gradual increase in knowledge that transforms financial novices into maestros. Encourage continuous learning, with readers becoming increasingly adept at navigating the financial score.

Enriching Financial Literacy: Showcase the enrichment that financial literacy brings to the symphony. Emphasize the importance of understanding financial terms, investment

strategies, and economic dynamics to compose a robust
financial knowledge base.

Reader Engagement: A Musical Interlude:

**Interactive Exercises: Break the rhythm with interactive
exercises, inviting readers to reflect on their personal
financial symphony. Prompt them to identify their financial
goals, evaluate their investment instruments, and design
their unique wealth-building dance.**

**Playlist of Financial Resources: Compile a "playlist" of
recommended financial resources—books, podcasts, and
online courses—that serve as the notes and melodies guiding
readers in their financial learning journey.**

Key Takeaways: A Harmonic Crescendo:

**Achieving Financial Harmony: Summarize the chapter with
the key takeaway of achieving financial harmony. Envision
readers conducting their financial orchestra with confidence,
creating a harmonious symphony that resonates with their
unique financial goals.**

**The Melody of a Balanced Life: Conclude by emphasizing
that the symphony of financial harmony extends beyond
numbers; it permeates every aspect of life. A balanced
financial life is akin to a well-composed melody, bringing joy,
security, and fulfillment.**

In crafting "The Symphony of Financial Harmony," Zohaib
Hassan Khan, our esteemed author, assumes the role of a
masterful conductor guiding readers through a mesmerizing
financial symphony. With each chapter, Khan orchestrates a
composition that goes beyond the realm of mere financial
advice. Instead, he artfully weaves together practical
wisdom, strategic insights, and a touch of inspiration to

create a harmonious melody that resonates with readers'
financial aspirations.

**1. Author as Maestro of Financial Wisdom:

Conducting the Financial Orchestra: Zohaib Hassan Khan
assumes the role of a maestro, conducting the financial
orchestra with expertise and finesse. His insights on
budgeting, investment, and wealth-building serve as the
notes that, when orchestrated thoughtfully, create a
symphony of financial success.

Guiding the Dance of Finances: In the ballet of budgeting
and the waltz of wealth-building, Khan's guidance is akin to
a dance instructor leading readers through each step.
Through his expert choreography, readers learn not only the
steps but also the elegance of financial maneuvers.

**2. The Maestro's Investment Overture:

Crafting Investment Crescendos: With an understanding of
investments comparable to a skilled conductor leading an
orchestra, Khan introduces readers to the investment
overture. He directs the instruments of stocks, bonds, and
mutual funds to create a harmonious crescendo of wealth
multiplication.

Showcasing the Beauty of Compounding: Like a maestro
emphasizing the beauty of a particular musical technique,

Khan emphasizes the significance of compound growth. Through his guidance, readers learn to appreciate the compound interest advantage, a melody that sweetens the financial journey over time.

**3. Waltzing to the Rhythm of Wealth Building:

Choreographing Financial Waltzes: As a choreographer of financial goals, Khan skillfully guides readers through the waltz of wealth building. Each financial goal becomes a graceful step in the dance, contributing to an overall performance of financial flourish.

Celebrating Financial Milestones: Much like a conductor signaling the orchestra to celebrate musical achievements, Khan encourages readers to celebrate their financial milestones. Whether it's achieving a savings goal or mastering an investment strategy, each milestone is a cause for celebration.

**4. Maestro of Financial Freedom Serenade:

Conducting the Serenade of Financial Freedom: In the serenade of financial freedom, Khan takes on the role of a conductor leading readers through the soothing melody of financial independence. Through strategic debt management and wealth-building strategies, he guides them to a symphony of financial liberation.

Eliminating Debt: A Harmonious Composition: Khan illustrates the symphony of debt freedom, turning each payment into a note in the composition of financial independence. Readers, under his guidance, learn to conduct their financial orchestra with the aim of creating a harmonious and debt-free future.

**5. The Maestro's Educational Crescendo:

Guiding the Educational Crescendo: As an advocate for continuous learning, Khan orchestrates the educational crescendo. Readers, following his lead, gradually increase their financial knowledge, transforming from novices to maestros of their financial score.

Enriching Financial Literacy:* Like a maestro enriching the musical repertoire, Khan enriches readers' financial literacy. By emphasizing the importance of understanding financial terms and investment strategies, he contributes to the creation of a robust financial knowledge base.

**6. Maestro's Notes on Reader Engagement:

Interactive Exercises as Musical Interludes: Khan introduces interactive exercises as musical interludes, inviting readers to actively participate in the financial performance. Through these exercises, readers engage with the financial symphony, making it a personalized and enriching experience.

Playlist of Financial Resources: By curating a "playlist" of recommended financial resources, Khan acts as a curator of musical notes. Each resource becomes a valuable note in the reader's financial composition, guiding them in their financial learning journey.

**7. Key Takeaways: A Harmonic Crescendo by the Maestro:

Achieving Financial Harmony:* As a maestro, Khan orchestrates the achievement of financial harmony. Through the harmonious symphony of financial elements, readers conduct their financial orchestra with confidence, creating a melody that resonates with their unique financial goals.

Balanced Life: The Melody's Finale:* The chapter concludes with the maestro reminding readers that the symphony of financial harmony extends beyond numbers. It permeates every aspect of life, creating a balanced and fulfilling melody that brings joy, security, and fulfillment.

Chapter 8: The Alchemy of Debt Management

<u>Transforming Financial Challenges into Wealth Opportunities</u>

In Chapter 8, Zohaib Hassan Khan delves into the alchemy of debt management, unraveling the intricate art of turning financial challenges into wealth-building opportunities. This chapter serves as a transformative guide, providing readers with actionable steps to navigate and conquer the complexities of debt. Khan, akin to a financial alchemist, empowers readers to transmute debt burdens into stepping stones toward financial prosperity.

**1. Understanding the Alchemy of Debt:

The Debt Alchemy Blueprint: Khan lays out the debt alchemy blueprint, demystifying the various forms of debt—credit cards, loans, mortgages—and their impact on financial well-being. Understanding the alchemy involves recognizing debt as both a challenge and an opportunity.

Debt's Dual Nature: Similar to alchemical elements having dual properties, debt can either be a hindrance or a tool for wealth creation. Khan guides readers in discerning the difference and harnessing the transformative potential of strategic debt management.

**2. Actions to Transmute High-Interest Debt:

Identifying High-Interest Debts: Like an alchemist seeking the purest elements, Khan instructs readers to identify high-interest debts. These debts, analogous to impurities, can hinder financial progress and need special attention for transmutation.

Consolidation and Negotiation:* Introducing alchemical practices, Khan guides readers in consolidating high-interest debts. By negotiating with creditors and potentially consolidating debts into a single, more manageable form,

readers begin the alchemical process of transforming
financial burdens.

Transmutation through Debt Repayment:* Khan emphasizes
the power of focused debt repayment as an alchemical
process. Readers learn actionable steps to allocate additional
funds to high-interest debts, accelerating the transmutation
of financial challenges into newfound financial strength.

**3. Alchemy of Leveraging Low-Interest Debt:

Discerning Low-Interest Opportunities:* Much like an
alchemist distinguishing between beneficial and harmful
elements, Khan instructs readers to discern low-interest debt
opportunities. Certain debts, such as mortgage loans or low-
interest credit, can be leveraged for wealth-building
purposes.

Strategic Use of Low-Interest Debt:* Readers are guided
through the strategic use of low-interest debt as an
alchemical tool. Whether for investing, home improvements,
or business endeavors, Khan illustrates how judicious use of
low-interest debt can lead to wealth creation.

**4. The Philosopher's Stone of Budgeting and Debt
Reduction:

Budgeting as the Philosopher's Stone:* Khan introduces
budgeting as the philosopher's stone—a powerful tool in the

alchemical process. Readers learn to wield budgeting as a transformative force, converting financial habits into gold, effectively reducing unnecessary expenses and freeing up funds for debt repayment.

Snowball and Avalanche Techniques:* Drawing inspiration from alchemical processes, Khan introduces the snowball and avalanche techniques for debt reduction. Readers discover how these strategies, when applied consistently, transmute small victories into significant financial achievements.

**5. Alchemy of Debt Consolidation and Negotiation:

Debt Consolidation Elixirs:* Khan introduces readers to debt consolidation elixirs, guiding them through the process of consolidating multiple debts into a single, more manageable form. This alchemical practice not only simplifies financial management but also reduces overall interest burdens.

Negotiation Potions:* As an alchemist concocting negotiation potions, Khan provides readers with effective negotiation strategies. Whether negotiating lower interest rates or more favorable repayment terms, readers learn to leverage their financial knowledge to enhance the alchemical process.

Reader Engagement: Participating in the Alchemical Transformation:

Alchemy Workshops:* Khan invites readers to participate in alchemy workshops, where they actively engage in budgeting exercises, debt consolidation simulations, and negotiation role-playing. These workshops become laboratories where readers practice the alchemy of debt management in a controlled and supportive environment.

Tracking Financial Transmutation:* Encouraging readers to track their financial transmutation, Khan introduces tools and techniques for monitoring progress. Much like an alchemical journal, tracking financial changes provides insights into the ongoing transformation of debt into wealth.

Key Takeaways: Mastery of Debt Alchemy:

Debt as a Transformative Medium:* Khan concludes the chapter by emphasizing the transformative nature of debt. When approached with knowledge and strategic action, debt becomes a medium for alchemical change, where financial challenges evolve into opportunities for wealth creation.

Becoming Debt Alchemists:* Readers, under Khan's guidance, become debt alchemists, equipped with the knowledge and tools to transmute financial challenges into wealth opportunities. The chapter empowers them to wield the alchemy of debt management, turning their financial situations into golden pathways toward prosperity.

Chapter 9: The Wealth Mindset Blueprint

Cultivating a Mindset for Prosperity and Abundance

In Chapter 9, Zohaib Hassan Khan unveils the Wealth Mindset Blueprint—a transformative guide that transcends traditional financial wisdom. As an architect of mental landscapes, Khan invites readers to explore the profound impact of mindset on financial success. This chapter serves as a beacon, illuminating the path toward cultivating a mindset that attracts prosperity and abundance.

**1. Understanding the Wealth Mindset:

The Mind's Blueprint:* Khan begins by explaining the mind's blueprint—the internal architecture that shapes beliefs, attitudes, and behaviors toward wealth. Readers discover the intricacies of how thoughts influence financial outcomes, laying the foundation for cultivating a wealth mindset.

Limiting Beliefs Identification:* Much like an architect identifying structural weaknesses, Khan guides readers in recognizing limiting beliefs around money. Through introspection, readers pinpoint thoughts and beliefs that may be hindering their financial growth.

**2. Actions for Rewiring Thought Patterns:

Affirmations as Mental Blueprints:* Khan introduces the concept of affirmations as mental blueprints for wealth. Readers learn actionable steps to create positive affirmations that reinforce abundance, prosperity, and financial success.

Visualization Techniques:* Instructing readers like a mental architect, Khan introduces visualization techniques. Readers embark on a journey of mentally constructing their desired financial future, allowing them to vividly imagine and manifest their goals.

Positive Language and Self-Talk:* like an architect refining the language of a blueprint, Khan emphasizes the importance of positive language and self-talk. Readers discover how subtle shifts in the way they speak about money can reshape their financial mindset.

**3. Building a Foundation of Financial Confidence:

Confidence as a Cornerstone:* Khan Positions confidence as a cornerstone of the wealth mindset. Through practical exercises, readers build a solid foundation of financial confidence, empowering them to make bold decisions and embrace opportunities.

Celebrating Financial Wins:* Encouraging readers to celebrate financial wins, Khan instills a mindset of acknowledgment and gratitude. Recognizing achievements, no matter how small, becomes a catalyst for reinforcing the wealth mindset?

**4. Embracing a Growth Mindset:

Growth Mindset as Dynamic Architecture:* Khan introduces the growth mindset as dynamic architecture, showcasing how the belief in continuous learning and adaptability contributes to financial success. Readers learn to embrace challenges as opportunities for growth.

Learning from Setbacks:* Like a mentor guiding architectural apprentices, Khan teaches readers to view setbacks as lessons in the construction process. Each challenge becomes a chance to refine and strengthen the structure of their wealth mindset.

**5. Cultivating Generosity and Abundance:

Generosity as Wealth Fertilizer:* Khan explores the transformative power of generosity. Readers discover how acts of giving, whether in time, knowledge, or resources, act as fertilizer for the growth of abundance and prosperity.

Abundance Mentality:* Instructing readers to adopt an abundance mentality, Khan leads them through exercises that shift their focus from scarcity to plenty. Cultivating gratitude for what they have opens the door to receiving more.

Reader Engagement: Blueprint Crafting Sessions:

Mindset Blueprint Crafting Sessions:* Khan invites readers to participate in mindset blueprint crafting sessions. These interactive exercises allow readers to actively shape their mental architecture, fostering an environment that attracts wealth and prosperity.

Peer Learning Circles:* Facilitating peer learning circles, Khan encourages readers to share their experiences and insights. These circles become supportive communities where individuals exchange ideas, strategies, and encouragement on their journey to cultivating a wealth mindset.

Key Takeaways: Blueprinting a Prosperous Future:

The Power of Mindset Blueprints:* Khan concludes the chapter by reinforcing the power of mindset blueprints in shaping financial destinies. The wealth mindset becomes a transformative force, guiding readers toward a future characterized by prosperity, abundance, and financial fulfillment.

Continued Blueprint Refinement:* Readers are inspired to view mindset cultivation as an ongoing process of blueprint refinement. By consistently shaping positive thought patterns, they create an enduring framework for a life of financial abundance.

Converting the insights from Chapter 9, "The Wealth Mindset Blueprint," into opportunities involves applying the principles of the wealth mindset to real-life scenarios. Here are practical steps to turn these insights into opportunities for personal and financial growth:

**1. Affirmations and Visualization in Goal Setting:

Opportunity: Leverage the power of affirmations and visualization to set and achieve financial goals.

Action Steps:

Craft affirmations that align with specific financial objectives.

Visualize the achievement of these goals regularly, reinforcing a positive mindset.

Translate the mental imagery into concrete action plans for wealth-building.

**2. Positive Language and Negotiation Skills:

Opportunity: Enhance negotiation skills and career advancement through positive language.

Action Steps:

Practice positive self-talk and language in professional interactions.

Participate in negotiation workshops or courses to develop and refine negotiation skills.

Use the wealth mindset to approach salary negotiations and career advancement discussions with confidence.

**3. Building Financial Confidence for Investment Opportunities:

Opportunity: Seize investment opportunities with a newfound sense of financial confidence.

Action Steps:

Identify investment opportunities aligned with personal financial goals.

Use the confidence gained from a wealth mindset to explore diverse investment options.

Seek guidance from financial advisors and actively engage in learning about investment strategies.

**4. Growth Mindset for Entrepreneurial Ventures:

Opportunity: Foster a growth mindset to explore and succeed in entrepreneurial ventures.

Action Steps:

Identify areas for personal and professional growth within the entrepreneurial landscape.

Embrace challenges as learning opportunities and view setbacks as stepping stones to success.

Connect with mentors and networks that support entrepreneurial endeavors, aligning with the growth mindset.

**5. Cultivating Generosity for Networking and Collaborations:

Opportunity: Use generosity as a tool for networking and collaborative opportunities.

Action Steps:

Engage in acts of generosity within professional and personal circles.

Explore networking events and platforms that align with the philosophy of abundance.

Foster collaborations by sharing knowledge, resources, and support within the community.

****6. Abundance Mentality in Financial Decision-Making:**

Opportunity: Apply the abundance mentality to make informed and confident financial decisions.

Action Steps:

Evaluate financial decisions with a focus on long-term abundance.

Avoid making decisions driven by scarcity or fear.

Seek out opportunities that align with the mindset of abundance, such as strategic investments or career moves.

****7. Blueprint Crafting Sessions for Personal Development:**

Opportunity: Participate in mindset blueprint crafting sessions for continuous personal development.

Action Steps:

Actively engage in personal development programs, workshops, and seminars.

Join or form peer learning circles to share insights and experiences.

Regularly revisit and refine the mindset blueprint to adapt to evolving goals and aspirations.

****8. Networking and Collaboration in Peer Learning Circles:**

Opportunity: Harness the power of peer learning circles for networking and collaboration.

Action Steps:

Actively participate in peer learning circles focused on wealth mindset and personal development.

Share experiences, challenges, and successes within the group.

Identify collaborative opportunities within the network, such as joint ventures or shared projects.

**9. Continuous Blueprint Refinement as a Habit:

Opportunity: Make continuous mindset blueprint refinement a habit for ongoing growth.

Action Steps:

Schedule regular reflections to assess mindset and adjust affirmations accordingly.

Embrace a mindset of continuous improvement in all aspects of life.

Cultivate a habit of seeking new opportunities aligned with evolving personal and financial goals.

By implementing these actions, readers can turn the wealth mindset blueprint into tangible opportunities for personal and financial development. The key is to apply the principles consistently and adapt them to various aspects of life, fostering a mindset that attracts abundance and propels individuals toward their desired outcomes.

Chapter 10: The Art of Strategic Networking

Building Relationships for Professional Growth and Opportunities

In Chapter 10, Zohaib Hassan Khan unveils "The Art of Strategic Networking," a guide to forging meaningful connections that extend beyond casual interactions. This chapter equips readers with the skills to build a robust professional network, opening doors to new opportunities, collaborations, and personal growth.

**1. Understanding the Essence of Networking:

Networking as Relationship Building:* Khan introduces networking as the art of relationship building, emphasizing the long-term benefits of genuine connections.

Action Steps:

Recognize the value of relationships beyond immediate gains.

Shift focus from transactional interactions to building authentic connections.

**2. Strategic Networking for Career Advancement:

Opportunity: Leverage strategic networking for career advancement and professional opportunities.

Action Steps:

Identify key individuals within the professional field and industry.

Attend industry-specific events and conferences to expand networks.

Engage in informational interviews to learn from experienced professionals.

**3. Effective Communication in Networking:

Building Communication Skills:* Khan highlights the importance of effective communication in networking success.

Action Steps:

Practice active listening during networking interactions.

Refine elevator pitches and personal stories for compelling communication.

Utilize non-verbal cues to enhance communication effectiveness.

**4. Building a Personal Brand for Networking Success:

Opportunity: Establish a strong personal brand to stand out in networking circles.

Action Steps:

Define personal strengths, values, and unique qualities.

Curate an online presence that reflects professional achievements and expertise.

Actively contribute to industry discussions and showcase thought leadership.

**5. Strategic Online Networking:

Expanding Opportunities through Online Platforms:* Khan explores the world of online networking and its potential for broader connections.

Action Steps:

Optimize professional profiles on platforms like LinkedIn.

Join industry-specific online forums and groups.

Actively participate in virtual events, webinars, and online discussions.

**6. Cultivating Reciprocal Relationships:

Opportunity: Cultivate reciprocal relationships for mutual benefit.

Action Steps:

Identify ways to provide value to network connections.

Offer support, resources, or knowledge to build trust.

Seek opportunities to collaborate and create win-win situations.

**7. Navigating Networking Events with Confidence:

Mastering In-Person Networking:* Khan guides readers in navigating in-person networking events with confidence.

Action Steps:

Set clear goals for each networking event.

Approach conversations with a genuine interest in others.

Follow up promptly with new connections to strengthen relationships.

**8. Expanding Networks through Mentorship:

Opportunity: Expand networks through mentorship and guidance.

Action Steps:

Identify potential mentors within the industry.

Approach mentorship as a two-way street, offering value in return.

Seek advice and guidance to accelerate personal and professional growth.

**9. Networking for Entrepreneurial Ventures:

Leveraging Networks for Business Growth:* Khan explores the role of networking in fostering entrepreneurial success.

Action Steps:

Attend industry-specific entrepreneurial events and meetups.

Collaborate with other entrepreneurs for joint ventures.

Utilize networks to access resources, investors, and potential clients.

**10. Continuous Network Maintenance:

Opportunity: Recognize the value of continuous network maintenance for sustained success.

Action Steps:

Regularly reach out to existing connections to maintain relationships.

Update professional profiles and achievements.

Actively participate in ongoing industry conversations and events.

Key Takeaways: Networking as a Lifelong Skill:

Networking as a Continuous Skill:* Khan concludes the chapter by emphasizing networking as a lifelong skill.

Action Steps:

Recognize that networking is an ongoing process, not a one-time activity.

Embrace networking as a tool for continuous learning and growth.

Cultivate a mindset of curiosity and openness in all networking endeavors.

By applying the principles outlined in "The Art of Strategic Networking," readers can transform networking into a strategic and fulfilling practice, unlocking opportunities for professional advancement, collaboration, and personal enrichment.

Networking is crucial for personal and professional success for several compelling reasons:

Opportunities for Career Advancement:

Job Opportunities: Networking provides access to a broader job market, connecting individuals with potential employers or job opportunities that may not be advertised publicly.

Career Guidance: Building relationships with experienced professionals allows for mentorship and valuable career advice, helping individuals navigate their career paths more effectively.

Knowledge Sharing and Learning:

Industry Insights: Networking enables individuals to stay updated on industry trends, news, and developments, providing valuable insights that contribute to professional growth.

Learning Opportunities: Engaging with a diverse network exposes individuals to different perspectives, experiences, and skill sets, fostering continuous learning and personal development.

Building a Strong Personal Brand:

Credibility: A well-established network can vouch for an individual's skills and expertise, enhancing their credibility in professional circles.

Visibility: Regular participation in industry events and online platforms increases an individual's visibility, contributing to the development of a strong personal brand.

Access to Resources and Support:

Resource Sharing: Networks facilitate the sharing of resources, whether in the form of information, contacts, or tools, fostering a collaborative environment.

Emotional Support: During challenging times, a supportive network provides emotional encouragement, advice, and solidarity, helping individuals navigate professional and personal difficulties.

Entrepreneurial Opportunities:

Partnerships and Collaborations: Entrepreneurs benefit significantly from networking by establishing partnerships, collaborations, and joint ventures that can fuel business growth.

Access to Investors: Networks provide access to potential investors, allowing entrepreneurs to secure funding for their ventures.

Increased Visibility in the Job Market:

Referrals: Networking often leads to referrals, with individuals recommending or introducing their connections to job opportunities, collaborators, or clients.

Market Presence: Being an active participant in industry-related events and discussions enhances an individual's visibility, making them more likely to be noticed by potential employers or collaborators.

Diverse Perspectives and Ideas:

Innovation: A diverse network brings together individuals with different backgrounds, experiences, and perspectives, fostering innovation and creativity.

Problem-Solving: When faced with challenges, a diverse network provides a pool of knowledge and ideas, offering varied approaches to problem-solving.

Professional Development and Mentorship:

Mentorship Opportunities: Networking opens doors to mentorship relationships, allowing individuals to learn from seasoned professionals and gain valuable insights.

Skill Enhancement: Interacting with professionals with diverse skill sets provides opportunities for skill enhancement and the development of new competencies.

Community and Social Connection:

Professional Community: Networking fosters a sense of belonging to a professional community, creating a support system and a sense of camaraderie.

Social Interaction: Engaging in networking events and activities provides social interaction, reducing professional isolation and enhancing overall well-being.

In essence, networking is not just about making connections; it's about cultivating meaningful relationships that contribute to personal and professional growth. The opportunities that arise from a well-nurtured network can be transformative, shaping careers, opening doors to new ventures, and providing a wealth of resources and support.

Chapter 11: Financial Intelligence Mastery

Navigating the Complexities of Personal Finance with Wisdom

In Chapter 11, Zohaib Hassan Khan explores the essence of "Financial Intelligence Mastery," guiding readers through the intricacies of personal finance. This chapter equips individuals with the knowledge and skills needed to make informed financial decisions, cultivate wealth, and secure a stable financial future.

**1. Understanding Financial Intelligence:

Financial Literacy as a Foundation:* Khan establishes financial literacy as the foundation of financial intelligence, emphasizing the importance of understanding financial concepts, terms, and principles.

Action Steps:

Commit to ongoing financial education through books, courses, and reputable online resources.

Seek clarity on basic financial concepts, such as budgeting, saving, investing, and debt management.

**2. Developing a Personal Budget:

Opportunity: Create a personal budget as a cornerstone of financial intelligence.

Action Steps:

Track income and expenses to gain insights into spending patterns.

Allocate funds strategically, prioritizing essential expenses and savings.

Regularly review and adjust the budget to align with financial goals.

**3. Effective Debt Management Strategies:

Opportunity: Implement effective debt management strategies to alleviate financial burdens.

Action Steps:

Identify and prioritize high-interest debts for repayment.

Explore debt consolidation options to streamline payments.

Negotiate with creditors for favorable terms and reduced interest rates.

**4. Investment Fundamentals:

Building Wealth through Investments:* Khan introduces the fundamentals of investing as a key aspect of financial intelligence.

Action Steps:

Understand different investment vehicles, including stocks, bonds, mutual funds, and real estate.

Diversify investment portfolios to manage risk.

Consult with financial advisors for personalized investment strategies.

**5. Smart Money Management Habits:

Cultivating Financial Discipline:* Khan emphasizes the importance of cultivating smart money management habits for long-term financial success.

Action Steps:

Practice disciplined spending and avoid impulse purchases.

Set financial goals and create actionable plans to achieve them.

Prioritize saving and investing as integral components of financial habits.

**6. Emergency Fund Creation:

Opportunity: Establish an emergency fund for financial resilience.

Action Steps:

Set a target amount for the emergency fund, typically covering three to six months' worth of living expenses.

Consistently contribute to the emergency fund until the target is reached.

Utilize the fund only for genuine emergencies to ensure financial stability.

**7. Insurance Planning for Protection:

Ensuring Financial Security:* Khan delves into the importance of insurance planning for safeguarding financial well-being.

Action Steps:

Assess insurance needs, including health, life, property, and disability insurance.

Regularly review and update insurance coverage to adapt to changing circumstances.

Seek professional advice to ensure comprehensive coverage.

**8. Retirement Planning Strategies:

Opportunity: Develop retirement planning strategies for a secure and comfortable future.

Action Steps:

Estimate retirement expenses and set realistic retirement goals.

Contribute consistently to retirement accounts, such as 401(k) or IRAs.

Explore investment options that align with long-term retirement objectives.

**9. Tax Optimization Techniques:

Minimizing Tax Liabilities:* Khan introduces tax optimization as an essential aspect of financial intelligence.

Action Steps:

Stay informed about tax laws and regulations to maximize deductions.

Utilize tax-advantaged accounts for savings and investments.

Consider consulting with tax professionals for personalized tax planning.

**10. Continuous Financial Education:

Opportunity: Embrace continuous financial education for ongoing mastery.

Action Steps:

Stay informed about economic trends, market conditions, and financial news.

Attend workshops, seminars, and webinars on evolving financial topics.

Join financial communities for knowledge-sharing and networking opportunities.

Key Takeaways: Empowering Financial Empowerment:

Financial Intelligence as Empowerment:* Khan concludes
the chapter by highlighting financial intelligence as a tool for
personal empowerment.

Action Steps:

Acknowledge the role of financial intelligence in achieving
financial goals and aspirations.

Commit to ongoing learning and implementation of sound
financial practices.

Recognize that financial intelligence is a lifelong journey
toward financial mastery and security.

The journey of Zohaib Hassan Khan, the author of
"Financial Intelligence Mastery," mirrors the principles
outlined in the chapter. Khan's personal experiences,
marked by ups and downs, underscore the significance of
financial intelligence in navigating life's uncertainties and
achieving long-term success.

**1. Resilience through Financial Literacy:

Author's Journey:* Zohaib Hassan Khan faced numerous
challenges and setbacks in his personal and professional life.

Relating to the Chapter:* His ability to overcome challenges
reflects the resilience cultivated through financial literacy.
Understanding financial concepts equipped him with the

knowledge needed to rebound from setbacks and make informed decisions.

**2. Strategic Budgeting Amidst Turbulence:

Author's Journey:* Khan's journey likely involved periods of financial turbulence where strategic budgeting became crucial.

Relating to the Chapter:* Creating a personal budget, as advocated in the chapter, allows individuals, including Khan, to manage financial resources effectively during uncertain times. By prioritizing essential expenses and saving strategically, one can weather financial storms more successfully.

**3. Debt Management as a Stepping Stone:

Author's Journey:* Like many, Khan might have faced challenges related to debt during his journey.

Relating to the Chapter:* The chapter's emphasis on effective debt management aligns with the idea that handling debt challenges can be a stepping stone to financial recovery. Negotiating favorable terms and prioritizing repayments contribute to long-term financial well-being.

**4. Investment Wisdom for Wealth Creation:

Author's Journey:* Khan's success likely involves wise investment decisions that contributed to wealth creation.

Relating to the Chapter:* Understanding investment fundamentals, diversifying portfolios, and seeking professional advice align with Khan's journey. The chapter's

principles emphasize how strategic investments play a
pivotal role in achieving financial goals.

**5. Discipline and Financial Habits:

Author's Journey:* Consistent discipline and financial habits
likely played a role in Khan's ability to persevere.

- The chapter advocates cultivating smart money
management habits, and Khan's journey is a testament to the
importance of discipline in financial matters. Establishing
and adhering to positive financial habits can lead to long-
term financial success.

**6. Emergency Fund for Stability:

Author's Journey:* Khan's experiences may have
underscored the importance of financial stability during
unexpected crises.

- The chapter's emphasis on creating an emergency fund
aligns with the idea that having a financial safety net
provides stability during challenging times. This principle
likely resonates with Khan's journey and the need for
preparedness.

**7. Insurance and Security:

Author's Journey:* Khan's understanding of financial
security may include the role of insurance in protecting
against unforeseen events.

- The chapter's inclusion of insurance planning reinforces the
idea that safeguarding financial well-being involves
anticipating and mitigating risks. Securing comprehensive

insurance coverage aligns with Khan's perspective on
financial security.

**8. Retirement Planning for a Secure Future:

Author's Journey:* Khan, like any individual, may prioritize
planning for a secure retirement.

- The chapter's focus on retirement planning corresponds
with the idea that securing one's financial future involves
setting realistic goals and consistently contributing to
retirement accounts. This aligns with the broader notion of
financial intelligence.

**9. Tax Optimization Strategies:

Author's Journey:* Khan likely recognizes the impact of tax
optimization on preserving income and wealth.

- The chapter's inclusion of tax optimization strategies
resonates with the concept that understanding and
leveraging tax laws contribute to financial well-being. It
aligns with Khan's likely approach to preserving financial
resources.

**10. Continuous Learning for Financial Mastery:

Author's Journey:* Khan's journey reflects the ongoing
pursuit of knowledge and adaptation to changing financial
landscapes.

- The chapter's emphasis on continuous financial education
aligns with the idea that financial mastery is a lifelong
journey. Khan's own commitment to learning and adapting

likely played a role in his ability to navigate challenges and achieve success.

In essence, Zohaib Hassan Khan's personal journey embodies the principles of financial intelligence highlighted in the chapter. His experiences demonstrate how cultivating financial literacy, making informed decisions, and embracing continuous learning contribute to resilience, success, and ultimately, financial empowerment.

Chapter 12: The Art of Negotiation Mastery

Unlocking Success through Effective Negotiation Skills

In Chapter 12, Zohaib Hassan Khan explores "The Art of Negotiation Mastery," unveiling the secrets to successful negotiations that transcend mere transactional exchanges. This chapter delves into the strategic and interpersonal aspects of negotiation, empowering readers to navigate diverse scenarios with finesse and achieve mutually beneficial outcomes.

**1. The Essence of Negotiation:

Negotiation as a Skill:* Khan establishes negotiation as a skill fundamental to personal and professional success, transcending mere deal-making.

Action Steps:

Recognize negotiation as an essential life skill, applicable in various contexts.

Embrace the mindset that negotiations are opportunities for collaboration rather than win-lose situations.

**2. Understanding the Psychology of Negotiation:

Human Dynamics in Negotiation:* Khan delves into the psychological aspects of negotiation, emphasizing the importance of understanding human behavior.

Action Steps:

Study and apply principles of behavioral psychology to better anticipate and influence negotiation dynamics.

Cultivate empathy and active listening to connect with negotiation counterparts on a human level.

**3. Building Rapport and Trust:

Foundation of Successful Negotiations:* Khan highlights the role of rapport and trust in negotiation success.

Action Steps:

Prioritize relationship-building and genuine connection before entering into negotiations.

Demonstrate authenticity and integrity to foster trust, laying the groundwork for collaborative discussions.

**4. Preparation and Information Mastery:

Opportunity:* Khan introduces negotiation preparation as a key opportunity for success.

Action Steps:

Thoroughly research and gather information about the negotiation counterpart and the subject matter.

Anticipate potential scenarios and objections, preparing responses and alternative solutions.

**5. Effective Communication Strategies:

Articulating Needs and Desires:* Khan explores the art of effective communication in negotiations.

Action Steps:

Develop clear and concise communication skills to articulate needs and desires.

Utilize verbal and non-verbal cues to convey confidence and assertiveness.

**6. Embracing Flexibility and Adaptability:

Opportunity:* Khan emphasizes the importance of flexibility and adaptability during negotiations.

Action Steps:

Be open to alternative solutions and compromises that align with overarching goals.

Readjust negotiation strategies based on real-time feedback and evolving circumstances.

**7. Overcoming Objections with Tact:

Navigating Challenges:* Khan guides readers in navigating objections with tact and diplomacy.

Action Steps:

Anticipate objections and prepare responses that address concerns without compromising core interests.

Transform objections into opportunities for collaborative problem-solving.

**8. Win-Win Negotiation Philosophy:

Philosophy of Collaboration:* Khan advocates for a win-win negotiation philosophy.

Action Steps:

Seek solutions that benefit all parties involved, fostering long-term relationships.

Prioritize collaboration over competition, recognizing that mutual success enhances overall satisfaction.

**9. Crisis and Conflict Resolution:

Turning Challenges into Opportunities:* Khan explores negotiation as a tool for crisis and conflict resolution.

Action Steps:

Approach conflicts with a problem-solving mindset, using negotiation as a constructive means of resolution.

Transform crises into opportunities for dialogue and collaboration.

**10. Continuous Improvement in Negotiation Skills:

Opportunity:* Khan concludes the chapter by encouraging continuous improvement in negotiation skills.

Action Steps:

Reflect on past negotiations to identify areas for improvement.

Engage in ongoing learning, such as workshops or courses, to refine negotiation techniques.

Seek feedback from counterparts to gain insights into one's negotiation style.

Key Takeaways: Navigating Life's Negotiations:

Negotiation as a Life Skill:* Khan emphasizes that negotiation is not confined to business dealings; it's a fundamental life skill.

Action Steps:

Recognize the applicability of negotiation in everyday life, from personal relationships to professional interactions.

Approach negotiations with a mindset of collaboration and the intention to build positive, enduring connections.

Chapter 13: The Power of Emotional Intelligence

Harnessing Emotions for Personal and Professional Success

In Chapter 13, Zohaib Hassan Khan delves into "The Power of Emotional Intelligence," unraveling the profound impact of understanding and managing emotions on individual success. This chapter explores the dimensions of emotional intelligence and provides practical insights for leveraging emotions as a powerful tool for personal and professional growth.

**1. Emotional Intelligence Defined:

Foundational Understanding:* Khan establishes the concept of emotional intelligence as the ability to recognize, understand, manage, and leverage emotions effectively.

Action Steps:

Develop self-awareness to recognize personal emotions and their impact.

Cultivate empathy to understand and resonate with the emotions of others.

**2. Self-Awareness Mastery:

Foundation of Emotional Intelligence:* Khan emphasizes self-awareness as the cornerstone of emotional intelligence.

Action Steps:

Engage in regular self-reflection to identify and understand personal emotions.

Recognize patterns of emotional responses in various situations.

**3. Empathy and Understanding Others:

Connection through Empathy:* Khan explores the role of empathy in connecting with and understanding others.

Action Steps:

Actively listen to others, seeking to understand their emotions and perspectives.

Put oneself in the shoes of others to foster deeper connections.

4. Effective Emotion Regulation:

Navigating Emotional Turbulence:* Khan guides readers in effectively regulating emotions, especially during challenging situations.

Action Steps:

Develop strategies for managing stress and maintaining emotional balance.

Practice mindfulness techniques to stay present and grounded.

5. Motivation through Emotional Alignment:

Opportunity:* Khan introduces emotional alignment as a catalyst for motivation and goal pursuit.

Action Steps:

Align personal goals with intrinsic motivations, tapping into the power of passion and enthusiasm.

Cultivate a positive emotional environment to fuel sustained motivation.

6. Social Skills and Relationship Building:

Building Strong Connections:* Khan explores the role of social skills in fostering meaningful relationships.

Action Steps:

Hone communication skills to express emotions clearly and authentically.

Foster collaborative environments through effective interpersonal interactions.

**7. Conflict Resolution with Emotional Intelligence:

Navigating Conflict successfully:* Khan guides readers in utilizing emotional intelligence for constructive conflict resolution.

Action Steps:

Approach conflicts with a calm and composed demeanor, focusing on finding solutions.

Use empathy to understand the emotions underlying conflicts and address them effectively.

**8. Leadership and Emotional Intelligence:

Leadership Impact:* Khan explores how emotional intelligence contributes to effective leadership.

Action Steps:

Lead with empathy, understanding the emotions and needs of team members.

Cultivate a positive emotional climate within the team, fostering collaboration and innovation.

**9. Resilience and Emotional Strength:

Opportunity:* Khan emphasizes the role of emotional intelligence in building resilience.

Action Steps:

Develop coping mechanisms to navigate challenges and setbacks.

View failures as opportunities for learning and growth, leveraging emotional strength.

**10. Continuous Growth in Emotional Intelligence:

Lifelong Development:* Khan concludes the chapter by encouraging continuous growth in emotional intelligence.

Action Steps:

Seek feedback from others to gain insights into emotional blind spots.

Engage in activities and practices that promote emotional well-being and intelligence.

Key Takeaways: Emotional Mastery for Success:

Emotional Intelligence as a Success Pillar:* Khan underscores emotional intelligence as a key factor in achieving personal and professional success.

Action Steps:

Embrace the power of emotions as a tool for self-discovery, connection, and resilience.

Commit to ongoing development in emotional intelligence, recognizing its transformative impact on various aspects of life.

Chapter 14: The Art of Effective Communication

Mastering the Language of Success

In Chapter 14, Zohaib Hassan Khan explores "The Art of Effective Communication," unveiling the transformative impact of clear and impactful communication on personal and professional success. This chapter delves into the nuances of communication, providing readers with practical insights and strategies to enhance their ability to convey ideas, build relationships, and navigate diverse communication scenarios.

**1. The Crucial Role of Communication:

Communication as a Foundation:* Khan establishes communication as a foundational element for success in various aspects of life.

Action Steps:

Recognize the pervasive impact of communication in personal and professional interactions.

Embrace the mindset that effective communication is a learnable skill that can be continuously improved.

**2. Clarity and Conciseness in Expression:

Power of Clear Expression:* Khan emphasizes the importance of clarity and conciseness in communication.

Action Steps:

Practice articulating ideas in a clear and straightforward manner.

Edit written communication to eliminate unnecessary complexity and ambiguity.

**3. Active Listening for Understanding:

Foundational Listening Skills:* Khan guides readers in developing active listening as a core component of effective communication.

Action Steps:

Cultivate the habit of truly listening to others, avoiding distractions and preconceived judgments.

Demonstrate understanding through verbal and non-verbal cues during conversations.

**4. Non-Verbal Communication Mastery:

The Language Beyond Words:* Khan explores the power of non-verbal cues in enhancing communication.

Action Steps:

Pay attention to body language, facial expressions, and gestures to convey authenticity and sincerity.

Align non-verbal communication with verbal messages to reinforce clarity.

**5. Adapting Communication Styles:

Opportunity:* Khan introduces the idea of adapting communication styles for diverse audiences.

Action Steps:

Assess the preferences and communication styles of different individuals or groups.

Flexibly adjust communication approaches to resonate with diverse audiences.

**6. Constructive Feedback and Critique:

Navigating Constructive Criticism:* Khan guides readers in providing and receiving feedback effectively.

Action Steps:

Offer feedback in a constructive and specific manner, focusing on behaviors rather than personal attributes.

Cultivate the ability to receive feedback with openness and a growth mindset.

**7. Conflict Resolution through Communication:

Turning Communication into Resolution:* Khan explores communication as a tool for resolving conflicts.

Action Steps:

Approach conflicts with a collaborative and solution-oriented mindset.

Use effective communication to understand differing perspectives and find common ground.

**8. Building Rapport and Connection:

Connection as a Communication Outcome:* Khan emphasizes the role of communication in building meaningful connections.

Action Steps:

Foster rapport through authentic and relatable communication.

Prioritize relationship-building in both personal and professional interactions.

**9. Public Speaking and Presentation Skills:

Opportunity:* Khan introduces the opportunity for success through effective public speaking and presentations.

Action Steps:

Develop and practice public speaking skills to convey ideas confidently.

Structure presentations to engage and captivate the audience effectively.

**10. Continuous Improvement in Communication:

Lifelong Development:* Khan concludes the chapter by encouraging continuous improvement in communication skills.

Action Steps:

Seek feedback from peers, mentors, or communication experts to identify areas for improvement.

Engage in ongoing learning, such as communication workshops or courses, to refine and expand communication abilities.

Key Takeaways: Communication as a Catalyst for Success:

Communication as a Skill Set:* Khan underscores that effective communication is a skill set that can be developed and refined.

Action Steps:

Recognize the transformative impact of clear and impactful communication on personal and professional success.

Commit to lifelong development in communication, understanding its pivotal role in achieving goals and fostering meaningful connections.

Chapter 15: **The Mindset of Resilience**

Bouncing Back from Adversity and Thriving in Challenges

In Chapter 15, Zohaib Hassan Khan explores "The Mindset of Resilience," shedding light on the transformative power of cultivating resilience in the face of adversity. This chapter delves into the components of a resilient mindset, providing practical insights and actionable strategies to navigate challenges, bounce back from setbacks, and thrive in the midst of difficulties.

**1. Defining Resilience:

Foundational Understanding:* Khan defines resilience as the ability to adapt, bounce back, and thrive despite facing challenges.

Action Steps:

Embrace the understanding that resilience is not a fixed trait but a skill that can be developed.

Acknowledge that challenges are a natural part of life, and resilience is the key to overcoming them.

**2. Building a Growth Mindset:

Foundation of Resilience:* Khan emphasizes the role of a growth mindset in cultivating resilience.

Action Steps:

Adopt a mindset that views challenges as opportunities for growth.

Embrace the belief that one's abilities and intelligence can be developed through dedication and hard work.

**3. Acceptance and Adaptability:

Power of Acceptance:* Khan explores the importance of accepting reality and adapting to change.

Action Steps:

Practice acceptance of situations beyond personal control.

Cultivate adaptability by seeking alternative solutions and adjusting strategies in response to challenges.

**4. Positive Self-Talk and Optimism:

Mindset Shaping Language:* Khan guides readers in harnessing the power of positive self-talk and optimism.

Action Steps:

Replace negative self-talk with affirmations and positive reinforcement.

Cultivate an optimistic outlook by focusing on strengths, solutions, and opportunities in challenging situations.

5. Cultivating Emotional Regulation:

Navigating Emotional Turbulence:* Khan emphasizes the importance of emotional regulation in building resilience.

Action Steps:

Develop self-awareness to recognize and understand emotional responses.

Employ healthy coping mechanisms to manage stress and maintain emotional balance.

6. Mindfulness and Present Moment Awareness:

Opportunity:* Khan introduces mindfulness as a tool for building resilience.

Action Steps:

Practice mindfulness techniques, such as meditation and deep breathing, to stay present and grounded.

Cultivate awareness of the present moment, reducing the impact of past regrets or future anxieties.

7. Seeking Support and Connection:

Strength in Community:* Khan explores the role of seeking support in resilience-building.

Action Steps:

Reach out to friends, family, or colleagues during challenging times.

Foster meaningful connections and build a support network that can provide encouragement and guidance.

**8. Learning from Setbacks:

Turning Challenges into Opportunities:* Khan guides readers in reframing setbacks as opportunities for learning.

Action Steps:

Reflect on setbacks to extract valuable lessons and insights.

View failures as stepping stones toward improvement and future success.

**9. Setting Realistic Goals:

Opportunity:* Khan emphasizes the importance of setting realistic and achievable goals.

Action Steps:

Break larger goals into smaller, manageable tasks.

Celebrate small victories, reinforcing a sense of accomplishment and progress.

**10. Continuous Growth and Resilience Cultivation:

Lifelong Development:* Khan concludes the chapter by encouraging continuous growth in resilience.

Action Steps:

Approach challenges with a mindset of continuous improvement.

Engage in activities that promote mental and emotional well-being, contributing to long-term resilience.

Key Takeaways: Resilience as a Dynamic Skill:

Resilience as a Lifelong Journey:* Khan underscores that resilience is not a static trait but a dynamic skill that can be developed and strengthened.

Action Steps:

Recognize the transformative power of a resilient mindset in navigating challenges and thriving in the face of adversity.

Commit to continuous growth and development in resilience, fostering the ability to bounce back and flourish in all aspects of life.

Imran Khan: A Resilient Journey to Leadership

Imran Ahmed Khan Niazi, the former Prime Minister of Pakistan, embodies the essence of resilience through his remarkable and enduring journey spanning 26 years. Imran Khan's life reflects the principles discussed in the chapter on resilience, showcasing how a resilient mindset can lead to triumph despite numerous challenges.

1. Defining Resilience:

Imran Khan's Perspective:* Imran Khan faced formidable challenges both in his cricketing career and political journey. His resilience was evident in his ability to adapt and thrive despite setbacks.

2. Building a Growth Mindset:

Growth amid Challenges:* Imran Khan's transition from a world-renowned cricketer to a political leader required a growth mindset. He viewed challenges not as obstacles but as opportunities for personal and national growth.

3. Acceptance and Adaptability:

Political Evolution:* Imran Khan navigated the complex and ever-changing political landscape in Pakistan. His resilience was reflected in his acceptance of political realities and his ability to adapt his strategies to the evolving political scenario.

4. Positive Self-Talk and Optimism:

Optimism in the Face of Adversity:* Imran Khan's speeches and public addresses often convey a sense of optimism and belief in the potential for positive change. His ability to maintain a positive self-talk narrative has been a source of inspiration for many.

5. Cultivating Emotional Regulation:

Steadfastness:* Imran Khan's calm demeanor and composed approach, especially in challenging situations, reflect emotional regulation. His resilience is evident in his ability to maintain emotional balance, even during political storms.

**6. Mindfulness and Present Moment Awareness:

Focused Leadership:* Imran Khan's leadership style emphasizes the importance of staying focused on the present moment. This mindfulness allows him to address immediate challenges while keeping a long-term vision for Pakistan's future.

**7. Seeking Support and Connection:

Building a Political Movement:* Imran Khan's success is not a solo effort; it involves the support of a dedicated political and social movement. His ability to connect with people and build a support network has been instrumental in his political journey.

**8. Learning from Setbacks:

Political Setbacks:* Imran Khan's political career faced numerous setbacks, from electoral defeats to legal challenges. Yet, each setback served as a learning opportunity, shaping his approach and strategies for the future.

**9. Setting Realistic Goals:

Vision for Pakistan:* Imran Khan's vision for a "Naya Pakistan" (New Pakistan) reflects the importance of setting realistic yet ambitious goals. His resilience is evident in his continuous pursuit of these goals despite the complexities of governance.

**10. Continuous Growth and Resilience Cultivation:

Evolution as a Leader:* Imran Khan's leadership journey has been marked by continuous growth and adaptation. His resilience is not a one-time achievement but a dynamic quality that evolves with each challenge faced.

In summary, Imran Khan's journey from a cricketing legend to a prominent political figure exemplifies the principles of resilience discussed in the chapter. His ability to bounce back, adapt to changing circumstances, and maintain a positive outlook showcases the transformative power of a resilient mindset. Imran Khan's life serves as an attractive testament to the enduring strength that resilience can bring to an individual's character and leadership.

Chapter 16: THE ART OF STRATEGIC DECISION-MAKING

Navigating Life's Crossroads with Foresight

In Chapter 16, Zohaib Hassan Khan explores "The Art of Strategic Decision-Making," unraveling the intricacies of making informed and impactful choices that shape personal and professional trajectories. This chapter delves into the key components of strategic decision-making, providing readers with practical insights and actionable strategies to enhance their ability to make sound and forward-thinking decisions.

**1. Decision-Making as a Skill:

Foundational Understanding:* Khan establishes decision-making as a skill that can be developed and refined.

Action Steps:

Embrace the mindset that decision-making is a learnable skill with lifelong implications.

Acknowledge the importance of strategic decision-making in achieving long-term goals.

**2. Clarity in Goals and Objectives:

Power of Clear Objectives:* Khan emphasizes the significance of setting clear goals and objectives before making decisions.

Action Steps:

Define short-term and long-term goals to provide a clear direction for decision-making.

Align decisions with overarching objectives to ensure consistency and coherence.

**3. Data-Driven Decision-Making:

Informed Choices:* Khan explores the role of data and information in making well-informed decisions.

Action Steps:

Gather relevant data and information before making significant decisions.

Utilize analytical tools and methodologies to assess the potential outcomes of choices.

**4. Risk Assessment and Mitigation:

Navigating Uncertainty:* Khan guides readers in assessing and mitigating risks associated with decisions.

Action Steps:

Identify potential risks and uncertainties associated with each decision.

Develop contingency plans to minimize the impact of unforeseen challenges.

**5. Stakeholder Analysis:

Considering Perspectives:* Khan emphasizes the importance of considering the perspectives of stakeholders in decision-making.

Action Steps:

Identify and analyze the interests and concerns of individuals or groups affected by the decision.

Seek feedback from relevant stakeholders to ensure a comprehensive understanding of potential implications.

**6. Strategic Thinking and Long-Term Vision:

Forward-Thinking Approach:* Khan explores the role of strategic thinking in decision-making.

Action Steps:

Cultivate a long-term vision that aligns with personal and professional aspirations.

Assess the potential impact of decisions on future goals and objectives.

**7. Decision Implementation Planning:

Execution Excellence:* Khan guides readers in developing robust plans for implementing decisions effectively.

Action Steps:

Create a step-by-step implementation plan detailing the actions required to execute the decision.

Anticipate potential challenges and establish monitoring mechanisms for ongoing assessment.

**8. Feedback Integration and Adaptation:

Learning from Experience:* Khan emphasizes the importance of incorporating feedback into the decision-making process.

Action Steps:

Solicit feedback from relevant sources and use it to refine decision-making strategies.

Cultivate adaptability, recognizing that decisions may need adjustments based on evolving circumstances.

**9. Ethical Decision-Making:

Integrity in Choices:* Khan explores the role of ethics in decision-making.

Action Steps:

Consider the ethical implications of decisions, ensuring alignment with personal values and principles.

Seek guidance from ethical frameworks and consult with trusted advisors when faced with ethical dilemmas.

**10. Continuous Improvement in Decision-Making:

Lifelong Development:* Khan concludes the chapter by encouraging continuous improvement in decision-making skills.

Action Steps:

Reflect on past decisions, analyzing both successes and failures for valuable insights.

Engage in ongoing learning, staying informed about decision-making methodologies and best practices.

Key Takeaways: Empowering Choices for Success:

Decision-Making as Empowerment:* Khan underscores that strategic decision-making is a powerful tool for personal and professional empowerment.

Action Steps:

Recognize the impact of decisions on overall success and well-being.

Commit to continuous development in decision-making, understanding its pivotal role in achieving goals and navigating life's complexities.

Chapter 17: The Science of Productivity Mastery

Unlocking Peak Performance in Personal and Professional Life

In Chapter 17, Zohaib Hassan Khan explores "The Science of Productivity Mastery," providing readers with valuable insights and practical strategies to optimize their efficiency and achieve peak performance. This chapter delves into the principles and techniques that contribute to enhanced productivity, empowering individuals to make the most of their time and resources.

**1. Productivity as a Fundamental Skill:

Foundational Understanding:* Khan establishes productivity as a foundational skill that underpins success in various endeavors.

Action Steps:

Embrace the mindset that productivity is a learnable skill that can be cultivated over time.

Acknowledge the direct correlation between effective productivity and achieving personal and professional goals.

**2. Goal Alignment and Prioritization:

Focus on Key Objectives:* Khan emphasizes the importance of aligning daily tasks with overarching goals and priorities.

Action Steps:

Define and prioritize short-term and long-term goals to guide daily activities.

Regularly assess tasks and activities, ensuring they contribute to the achievement of strategic objectives.

**3. Time Management Strategies:

Efficient Time Utilization:* Khan explores various time management techniques to maximize efficiency.

Action Steps:

Adopt time-blocking methods to allocate specific time slots for different tasks.

Utilize productivity tools and apps to organize schedules and set reminders.

**4. Effective Task Delegation:

Leveraging Team Resources:* Khan guides readers in mastering the art of delegating tasks to optimize efficiency.

Action Steps:

Identify tasks that can be effectively delegated to others.

Develop clear communication channels and expectations when assigning tasks to team members.

**5. Mindfulness and Focus:

Present Moment Engagement:* Khan emphasizes the role of mindfulness in enhancing focus and concentration.

Action Steps:

Practice mindfulness techniques, such as meditation or deep breathing, to enhance concentration.

Minimize multitasking and dedicate focused attention to one task at a time.

**6. Optimizing Workspace and Environment:

Setting the Stage for Productivity:* Khan explores the impact of a conducive workspace on overall efficiency.

Action Steps:

Organize the workspace for optimal functionality and minimal distractions.

Cultivate a work environment that inspires creativity and focus.

**7. Effective Communication for Efficiency:

Streamlining Communication:* Khan guides readers in improving communication processes to reduce time wastage.

Action Steps:

Streamline communication channels, avoiding unnecessary meetings or lengthy emails.

Utilize concise and clear communication methods to convey information effectively.

**8. Continuous Learning and Skill Development:

Adapting to Evolving Needs:* Khan emphasizes the importance of continuous learning to stay ahead in a rapidly changing environment.

Action Steps:

Invest time in ongoing skill development relevant to personal and professional objectives.

Stay informed about industry trends and advancements to proactively adapt to evolving requirements.

**9. Strategic Use of Technology:

Leveraging Tools for Efficiency:* Khan explores how technology can enhance productivity when used strategically.

Action Steps:

Evaluate and incorporate productivity tools that align with specific needs and preferences.

Stay updated on emerging technologies that can streamline tasks and processes.

**10. Wellness and Work-Life Balance:

Holistic Approach to Productivity:* Khan concludes the chapter by highlighting the importance of wellness in maintaining sustained productivity.

Action Steps:

Prioritize self-care, including regular exercise, adequate sleep, and healthy nutrition.

Establish boundaries to maintain a healthy work-life balance and prevent burnout.

Key Takeaways: Mastering Efficiency for Success:

Productivity as a Lifestyle:* Khan underscores that productivity is not just a set of techniques but a holistic lifestyle that contributes to overall success.

Action Steps:

Internalize the belief that productivity mastery is within reach through consistent effort and continuous improvement.

Cultivate a proactive approach to efficiency, making intentional choices that align with personal and professional aspirations.

Chapter 18: THE ART OF EFFECTIVE NETWORKING

Building Meaningful Connections for Professional Success

In Chapter 18, Zohaib Hassan Khan explores "The Art of Effective Networking," providing readers with insights and strategies to cultivate meaningful connections that contribute to personal and professional success. This chapter delves into the principles of networking, offering practical advice to enhance networking skills and leverage connections for growth and opportunities.

**1. Networking as a Strategic Skill:

Foundational Understanding:* Khan establishes networking as a strategic skill essential for personal and professional growth.

Action Steps:

Embrace the mindset that networking is not just about quantity but quality in building connections.

Recognize the long-term value of networking in creating opportunities and fostering collaborations.

**2. Clarifying Networking Goals:

Intentional Connection Building:* Khan emphasizes the importance of setting clear goals when engaging in networking activities.

Action Steps:

Define specific objectives, such as expanding industry knowledge, finding mentors, or exploring career opportunities.

Tailor networking efforts to align with individual goals and aspirations.

**3. Strategic Event Selection:

Optimizing Networking Opportunities:* Khan guides readers in selecting and participating in events strategically.

Action Steps:

Identify events relevant to personal or professional interests.

Plan attendance at conferences, seminars, or industry gatherings with a focus on meaningful engagement.

4. Effective Communication in Networking:

Building Rapport:* Khan explores the role of effective communication in establishing and nurturing connections.

Action Steps:

Develop an authentic and compelling personal narrative for networking introductions.

Actively listen to others, expressing genuine interest in their experiences and perspectives.

5. Utilizing Online Platforms:

Digital Networking Excellence:* Khan discusses the significance of leveraging online platforms for networking.

Action Steps:

Optimize professional profiles on platforms like LinkedIn, highlighting skills, achievements, and goals.

Engage in meaningful conversations and contribute value to online communities within the respective industry.

6. Reciprocity and Relationship Building:

**Fostering Mutually Beneficial Connections:* Khan
emphasizes the importance of reciprocity in building lasting
relationships.

Action Steps:

Identify ways to contribute value to others in the network,
fostering a sense of mutual benefit.

Cultivate long-term relationships by staying connected and
offering support when possible.

7. Effective Follow-Up:

Sustaining Connections:* Khan guides readers in mastering
the art of effective follow-up after initial interactions.

Action Steps:

Send personalized follow-up messages expressing
appreciation for the connection.

Maintain regular communication to nurture relationships
over time.

8. Building a Diverse Network:

Expanding Perspectives:* Khan explores the advantages of
having a diverse and inclusive professional network.

Action Steps:

Actively seek connections with individuals from diverse
backgrounds, industries, and perspectives.

Attend networking events that promote inclusivity and
diversity.

**9. Seeking and Offering Mentorship:

Mentorship Dynamics:* Khan highlights the significance of seeking and offering mentorship within the network.

Action Steps:

Identify potential mentors based on expertise and experience.

Be open to mentoring others, contributing to the growth of the network.

**10. Continuous Network Cultivation:

Lifelong Development:* Khan concludes the chapter by encouraging continuous cultivation and expansion of the professional network.

Action Steps:

Regularly reassess networking goals and adjust strategies accordingly.

Actively participate in industry events, forums, and discussions to stay connected and informed.

Key Takeaways: Networking for Long-Term Success:

Strategic Relationship Building:* Khan underscores that effective networking is a strategic skill with long-term benefits for personal and professional success.

Action Steps:

Embrace networking as a dynamic and ongoing process that requires intentional effort and continuous improvement.

Cultivate a network that adds value, fosters collaboration, and contributes to individual and collective growth.

"Networking is not just about exchanging business cards; it's about cultivating relationships that stand the test of time and contribute to mutual growth."

"In the world of professional connections, quality surpasses quantity. Focus on building meaningful relationships that elevate both you and your network."

"Effective networking is a dance of reciprocity, where each step taken to support others echoes in the harmony of collective success."

"Your online presence is your virtual handshake. Optimize your digital footprint for networking success, turning connections into collaborations."

Chapter 19: The Art of Persuasion and Influential Communication

Mastering the Power of Persuasion for Success

In Chapter 19, Zohaib Hassan Khan explores "The Art of Persuasion and Influential Communication," unraveling the dynamics of persuasive communication that can shape opinions, drive decisions, and foster success. This chapter delves into the principles and techniques of persuasion, offering practical guidance on how to communicate effectively and influence others positively.

**1. Persuasion as a Core Skill:

Foundational Understanding:* Khan establishes persuasion as a fundamental skill for personal and professional success.

Action Steps:

Embrace the belief that effective communication is not just about conveying information but about inspiring action.

Acknowledge the ethical responsibility that comes with the power of persuasion.

**2. Understanding Your Audience:

Tailoring Messages for Impact:* Khan emphasizes the importance of knowing your audience to craft persuasive messages.

Action Steps:

Conduct audience analysis to understand their needs, interests, and perspectives.

Adapt communication styles to resonate with diverse audiences.

**3. Clarity and Simplicity in Communication:

Power of Clear Messaging:* Khan explores the impact of clear and simple communication in persuasive efforts.

Action Steps:

Craft messages with clarity, avoiding jargon and unnecessary complexity.

Use compelling and relatable examples to illustrate key points.

**4. Building Credibility and Trust:

Foundation of Persuasion:* Khan guides readers in establishing credibility as a cornerstone of persuasive communication.

Action Steps:

Demonstrate expertise and authenticity to build trust with your audience.

Uphold ethical standards to maintain long-term credibility.

**5. Emotional Appeal and Connection:

Inspiring Action through Emotion:* Khan explores the role of emotion in persuasive communication.

Action Steps:

Connect emotionally with your audience by incorporating relatable stories and experiences.

Appeal to positive emotions to inspire enthusiasm and commitment.

**6. Using Social Proof and Authority:

Influencing through Evidence:* Khan guides readers in leveraging social proof and authority to enhance persuasive efforts.

Action Steps:

Incorporate testimonials, case studies, and success stories to provide evidence of your message.

Establish and highlight relevant credentials or expertise to reinforce your authority.

**7. Creating a Sense of Urgency:

Motivating Timely Action:* Khan emphasizes the importance of instilling a sense of urgency in persuasive communication.

Action Steps:

Clearly communicate the time-sensitive nature of the message or call to action.

Utilize limited-time offers or opportunities to prompt immediate responses.

**8. Active Listening for Influence:

Building Influence through Listening:* Khan explores how active listening contributes to persuasive communication.

Action Steps:

Listen attentively to the concerns and perspectives of your audience.

Demonstrate understanding by incorporating their viewpoints into your messages.

**9. Handling Objections and Concerns:

Navigating Resistance:* Khan guides readers in addressing objections and concerns effectively.

Action Steps:

Anticipate potential objections and proactively address them in your communication.

Foster an open and collaborative environment for addressing concerns.

**10. Continuous Improvement in Persuasion:

Lifelong Development:* Khan concludes the chapter by encouraging continuous refinement of persuasive communication skills.

Action Steps:

Seek feedback from others to identify areas for improvement in your persuasive efforts.

Engage in ongoing learning, such as workshops or courses, to enhance your influence and communication abilities.

Key Takeaways: Persuasion as a Catalyst for Impact:

Persuasion as a Leadership Tool:* Khan underscores the transformative power of persuasive communication in leadership and decision-making.

Action Steps:

Recognize the ethical responsibility that comes with the ability to influence others.

Commit to continuous development in persuasive communication, understanding its pivotal role in achieving personal and professional goals.

Chapter 20: The Entrepreneurial Mindset

Cultivating Innovation and Resilience for Business Success

In Chapter 20, Zohaib Hassan Khan delves into "The Entrepreneurial Mindset," exploring the foundational principles and habits that drive entrepreneurial success. This chapter provides readers with insights into adopting an entrepreneurial mindset, fostering innovation, and navigating challenges to build successful ventures.

**1. Entrepreneurship as a Mindset:

Foundational Understanding:* Khan establishes that entrepreneurship is more than a business venture; it's a mindset that fuels innovation and resilience.

Action Steps:

Embrace the mindset that sees challenges as opportunities for innovation and growth.

Cultivate a passion for creating value and solving problems in unique ways.

**2. Visionary Goal Setting:

Setting Ambitious Targets:* Khan emphasizes the importance of visionary goal-setting in entrepreneurial endeavors.

Action Steps:

Set ambitious, yet achievable, long-term goals that align with your entrepreneurial vision.

Break down larger goals into actionable steps for strategic implementation.

**3. Risk-Taking and Fear Management:

Calculated Risk-Taking:* Khan guides readers in navigating the balance between risk-taking and fear management.

Action Steps:

Evaluate risks systematically, making informed decisions while embracing a calculated level of risk.

Develop resilience to manage fear and setbacks inherent in entrepreneurial pursuits.

**4. Innovative Problem Solving:

Creativity in Action:* Khan explores the entrepreneurial approach to innovative problem-solving.

Action Steps:

Cultivate a mindset that views problems as opportunities for creative solutions.

Encourage a culture of innovation within your entrepreneurial endeavors.

**5. Adaptability and Market Dynamics:

Navigating Change:* Khan emphasizes the importance of adaptability in the ever-evolving market landscape.

Action Steps:

Stay informed about market trends and be ready to adapt strategies based on changing dynamics.

Foster a culture of continuous improvement and agility within your entrepreneurial team.

**6. Resource Optimization:

Efficient Resource Management:* Khan guides readers in optimizing resources effectively in entrepreneurial ventures.

Action Steps:

Prioritize and allocate resources strategically based on the most impactful activities.

Seek creative solutions and partnerships to maximize
resource efficiency.

**7. Customer-Centric Approach:

Building for the Customer:* Khan explores the significance
of a customer-centric approach in entrepreneurial success.

Action Steps:

Prioritize understanding and meeting the needs of your
target audience.

Solicit and integrate customer feedback into product/service
development.

**8. Building a Resilient Team:

Team Dynamics in Entrepreneurship:* Khan emphasizes the
role of a resilient and motivated team in entrepreneurial
ventures.

Action Steps:

Foster a positive and collaborative team culture that
encourages innovation.

Invest in team development and provide support during
challenging times.

**9. Financial Literacy and Sustainability:

Smart Financial Management:* Khan guides readers in
adopting financial literacy for sustainable entrepreneurial
ventures.

Action Steps:

Develop a sound financial strategy and monitor key financial indicators.

Cultivate a mindset of long-term sustainability and fiscal responsibility.

**10. Continuous Learning and Growth:

Lifelong Entrepreneurial Development:* Khan concludes the chapter by encouraging continuous learning and personal growth.

Action Steps:

Embrace entrepreneurship as a journey of continuous learning and adaptation.

Stay curious, seek mentorship, and engage in ongoing entrepreneurial education.

Key Takeaways: Entrepreneurship as a Mindset for Success:

Mindset as the Driver:* Khan underscores that entrepreneurship is not just about starting businesses; it's a mindset that drives innovation, resilience, and success.

Action Steps:

Internalize the entrepreneurial mindset, embracing challenges as opportunities and continually seeking ways to create value.

Commit to lifelong entrepreneurial development, understanding that success is a dynamic and ever-evolving journey.

NOTE FROM AUTHOR

"I want to extend my heartfelt gratitude for embarking on this expedition of self-discovery and personal development. Your commitment to exploring these chapters demonstrates a dedication to positive change and growth, and for that, I am truly thankful.

Throughout these chapters, we've delved into the essential habits that can pave the way for a life of abundance, success, and fulfillment. From adopting the mindset of millionaires to mastering the art of persuasion, each chapter has been crafted to empower you with actionable insights that, when implemented, have the potential to bring about significant shifts in your life.

I want to express my admiration for your commitment to personal development. It takes courage to embrace change and embark on a journey of self-improvement. By completing these chapters, you've shown not only a willingness to learn but also a determination to apply these lessons to your life.

Remember, these habits are not just principles to be read and forgotten; they are tools meant to be wielded in the workshop of your daily life. As you step forward armed with this knowledge, I encourage you to integrate these habits into your routine, experiment with them, and witness the positive impact they can have.

May the entrepreneurial mindset, the art of persuasion, and the other habits discussed within these pages serve as catalysts for transformative change? I believe in your potential to create a life of purpose, success, and prosperity.

Thank you for entrusting me as your guide on this journey. I look forward to hearing about the incredible strides you make and the positive changes you bring into your life.

With gratitude and anticipation,

Zohaib Hassan Khan

Chapter 21: The Power of Gratitude and Positive Affirmations

Cultivating a Positive Mindset for Abundance

In Chapter 21, Zohaib Hassan Khan explores "The Power of Gratitude and Positive Affirmations," unraveling the profound impact these practices can have on one's mindset and overall well-being. This chapter delves into the transformative nature of gratitude and positive affirmations, offering practical insights and actionable steps to foster a positive outlook and attract abundance.

**1. Gratitude as a Daily Practice:

Foundational Understanding:* Khan establishes gratitude as a powerful daily practice that shifts focus towards positivity.

Action Steps:

Begin each day by reflecting on and expressing gratitude for the blessings in your life.

Maintain a gratitude journal to record moments of appreciation and reflection.

**2. Positive Affirmations for Self-empowerment:

Harnessing the Power of Words:* Khan explores the impact of positive affirmations on self-empowerment and mindset.

Action Steps:

Create a list of positive affirmations that align with your goals and aspirations.

Repeat these affirmations regularly to reinforce positive beliefs about yourself and your potential.

**3. Shifting Focus from Scarcity to Abundance:

Mindset Transformation:* Khan guides readers in shifting from a scarcity mindset to an abundance mindset.

Action Steps:

Identify and challenge limiting beliefs related to scarcity.

Cultivate an abundance mindset by acknowledging opportunities and possibilities.

**4. Expressing Gratitude in Relationships:

Strengthening Connections:* Khan emphasizes the role of gratitude in nurturing positive relationships.

Action Steps:

Express appreciation to friends, family, and colleagues regularly.

Foster a culture of gratitude within your personal and professional relationships.

**5. Using Affirmations for Goal Achievement:

Goal-oriented Positivity:* Khan explores how affirmations can support the achievement of specific goals.

Action Steps:

Align affirmations with your short-term and long-term goals.

Repeat affirmations related to success, resilience, and accomplishment.

**6. Gratitude as a Resilience Tool:

Building Emotional Strength: Khan guides readers in using gratitude as a tool for resilience during challenges.

Action Steps:

Find moments of gratitude even in difficult situations.

Use gratitude to reframe challenges as opportunities for growth.

****7. Affirmations for Confidence Building:**

Confidence Boost: Khan explores the role of affirmations in building and maintaining self-confidence.

Action Steps:

Create affirmations that reinforce your confidence and self-worth.

Repeat these affirmations regularly, especially in moments of self-doubt.

****8. Cultivating a Grateful Workplace:**

Positive Organizational Culture: Khan emphasizes the impact of gratitude on workplace morale and productivity.

Action Steps:

Encourage a culture of gratitude within your workplace.

Recognize and appreciate the efforts of colleagues and team members.

****9. Daily Affirmation Rituals:**

Integration into Daily Routine:* Khan guides readers in establishing daily rituals for affirmations.

Action Steps:

Set aside dedicated time each day for affirmations.

Create a ritual that integrates affirmations seamlessly into your routine.

10. Gratitude and Affirmations as Lifestyle Choices:

Life-long Habits:* Khan concludes the chapter by emphasizing the transformational nature of gratitude and affirmations as lifestyle choices.

Action Steps:

Internalize gratitude and affirmations as ongoing practices for a positive and fulfilling life.

Share the benefits of these practices with others, fostering a ripple effect of positivity.

Key Takeaways: Harnessing Positivity for Abundance:

Gratitude and Affirmations as Tools:* Khan underscores the profound impact of gratitude and positive affirmations as tools for cultivating a positive mindset and attracting abundance.

Action Steps:

Embrace gratitude and affirmations as transformative practices that contribute to a fulfilling and abundant life.

Integrate these habits into your daily routine, allowing them to shape your mindset and attract positivity.

Chapter 22: FINANCIAL INTELLIGENCE AND WEALTH BUILDING STRATEGIES

Empowering Your Financial Journey

In Chapter 22, Zohaib Hassan Khan explores "Financial Intelligence and Wealth Building Strategies," providing readers with essential insights and strategies to enhance their understanding of finances and lay the groundwork for building long-term wealth. This chapter delves into the

principles of financial intelligence, offering actionable steps
to make informed decisions and achieve financial goals.

**1. Foundations of Financial Intelligence:

Understanding the Basics:* Khan establishes the importance
of financial intelligence as the cornerstone of wealth building.

Action Steps:

Educate yourself on fundamental financial concepts,
including budgeting, saving, and investing.

Seek out reputable sources for financial education and stay
informed about economic trends.

**2. Budgeting for Financial Success:

Strategic Money Management:* Khan guides readers in
creating and maintaining a budget for effective financial
management.

Action Steps:

Develop a comprehensive budget that outlines income,
expenses, and savings goals.

Regularly review and adjust your budget to align with
changing financial circumstances.

**3. The Power of Saving and Investing:

Building Wealth Over Time:* Khan explores the significance
of saving and investing as key wealth-building strategies.

Action Steps:

Establish an emergency fund for unexpected expenses.

Explore various investment options, such as stocks, bonds, and real estate, based on your financial goals and risk tolerance.

**4. Debt Management and Financial Freedom:

Strategies for Debt Reduction:* Khan emphasizes the importance of managing and eliminating debt on the path to financial freedom.

Action Steps:

Develop a plan to pay off high-interest debts systematically.

Prioritize debt reduction while building a solid financial foundation.

**5. Understanding Credit and Its Impact:

Credit as a Financial Tool:* Khan guides readers in understanding the role of credit and maintaining a healthy credit score.

Action Steps:

Regularly check your credit report for accuracy and address any discrepancies.

Use credit responsibly and strategically to build a positive credit history.

**6. Diversification and Risk Management:

Building a Robust Portfolio:* Khan explores the principles of diversification and risk management in investment strategies.

Action Steps:

Diversify your investment portfolio across different asset classes to mitigate risk.

Periodically reassess and rebalance your portfolio based on changing market conditions.

**7. Tax Planning for Financial Optimization:

Maximizing Tax Efficiency:* Khan emphasizes the importance of tax planning to optimize financial outcomes.

Action Steps:

Stay informed about tax laws and regulations that impact your financial situation.

Explore tax-efficient investment strategies and take advantage of available deductions.

**8. Building Multiple Income Streams:

Financial Resilience:* Khan guides readers in exploring and developing multiple income streams for financial resilience.

Action Steps:

Identify opportunities to diversify your income, such as side businesses, investments, or passive income streams.

Continuously assess and expand your income-generating avenues.

**9. Long-Term Planning and Retirement:

Strategies for Retirement Security:* Khan explores long-term financial planning, with a focus on retirement.

Action Steps:

Set specific retirement goals and regularly reassess your progress.

Consider contributing to retirement accounts and exploring investment options that align with your retirement timeline.

**10. Continual Financial Education:

Lifelong Financial Literacy:* Khan concludes the chapter by highlighting the importance of continual financial education.

Action Steps:

Commit to ongoing financial education through books, courses, and reputable financial advisors.

Stay adaptive to changing economic conditions and adjust your financial strategies accordingly.

Key Takeaways: Navigating the Path to Financial Empowerment:

Financial Intelligence as Empowerment:* Khan underscores that financial intelligence is the key to making informed decisions and building lasting wealth.

Action Steps:

Embrace financial education as a lifelong journey, empowering yourself to navigate the complex landscape of personal finance.

Implement sound financial strategies to achieve your goals
and build a secure and prosperous future.

Chapter 23: **The Art of Time Management and Productivity**

Maximizing Efficiency for Optimal Results

In Chapter 23, Zohaib Hassan Khan explores "The Art of
Time Management and Productivity," providing readers
with invaluable insights and strategies to make the most of
their time and optimize productivity. This chapter delves
into effective time management techniques and productivity
principles, offering actionable steps to enhance efficiency and
achieve optimal results.

**1. Understanding the Value of Time:

Foundational Awareness:* Khan establishes the profound impact of time on personal and professional success.

Action Steps:

Reflect on the value of time in achieving your goals and aspirations.

Prioritize tasks based on their contribution to long-term objectives.

**2. Setting Clear Goals and Priorities:

Strategic Objective Alignment:* Khan guides readers in aligning daily tasks with overarching goals for effective time management.

Action Steps:

Define and prioritize short-term and long-term goals to guide daily activities.

Regularly assess tasks and activities to ensure they contribute to the achievement of strategic objectives.

**3. Effective Planning Techniques:

Strategies for Efficient Planning:* Khan explores various planning techniques to enhance organizational skills.

Action Steps:

Implement time-blocking methods to allocate specific time slots for different tasks.

Utilize productivity tools and apps to organize schedules and set reminders.

4. Delegation for Optimal Efficiency:

Leveraging Team Resources:* Khan guides readers in mastering the art of delegating tasks for optimal efficiency.

Action Steps:

Identify tasks that can be effectively delegated to others.

Develop clear communication channels and expectations when assigning tasks to team members.

5. Mindfulness and Focus:

Present Moment Engagement:* Khan emphasizes the role of mindfulness in enhancing focus and concentration.

Action Steps:

Practice mindfulness techniques, such as meditation or deep breathing, to enhance concentration.

Minimize multitasking and dedicate focused attention to one task at a time.

6. Optimizing Workspace and Environment:

Setting the Stage for Productivity:* Khan explores the impact of a conducive workspace on overall efficiency.

Action Steps:

Organize the workspace for optimal functionality and minimal distractions.

Cultivate a work environment that inspires creativity and focus.

7. Effective Communication for Efficiency:

Streamlining Communication:* Khan guides readers in improving communication processes to reduce time wastage.

Action Steps:

Streamline communication channels, avoiding unnecessary meetings or lengthy

Prioritize important decisions earlier in the day when cognitive resources are plentiful.

Implement routines and automate certain decisions to reduce decision fatigue.

**5. Group Decision Dynamics:

Navigating Collective Decision Making:* Khan explores the dynamics of decision making in group settings.

Action Steps:

Foster open communication and encourage diverse perspectives in group decision-making processes.

Implement structured decision-making frameworks to enhance group efficiency.

**6. Learning from Decision Outcomes:

Adaptive Decision-Making:* Khan guides readers in learning from both successful and unsuccessful decision outcomes.

Action Steps:

Conduct regular reviews of decision outcomes to identify patterns and areas for improvement.

Embrace a growth mindset that views failures as opportunities for learning and refinement.

**7. Decision-Making in Uncertainty:

Strategies for Ambiguous Situations:* Khan provides insights into making decisions when faced with uncertainty.

Action Steps:

Gather as much relevant information as possible before making decisions.

Develop contingency plans and flexibility to adapt to changing circumstances.

**8. Avoiding Decision Paralysis:

Overcoming Decision-Making Hurdles:* Khan explores strategies to overcome decision paralysis.

Action Steps:

Break down complex decisions into smaller, manageable tasks.

Set realistic deadlines for decision-making processes to prevent procrastination.

**9. Ethical Decision Making:

Integrity in Choices:* Khan emphasizes the importance of ethical considerations in decision making.

Action Steps:

Establish a personal code of ethics to guide decision-making processes.

Consider the long-term consequences and ethical implications of decisions.

**10. Continuous Improvement in Decision Making:

Lifelong Decision-Making Development:* Khan concludes the chapter by highlighting the journey of continuous improvement in decision making.

Action Steps:

Embrace decision making as a skill that can be honed and refined over time.

Seek feedback and actively engage in learning opportunities to enhance decision-making capabilities.

Key Takeaways: Mastering the Art of Decision Making:

Decision Making as a Skill:* Khan underscores that decision making is not just a process but a skill that can be developed and improved.

Action Steps:

Approach decision making with intentionality, considering psychological factors and implementing strategies for continuous improvement.

Cultivate a mindset that views decisions as opportunities for growth and refinement, contributing to overall personal and professional success.

Chapter 25: Building and Nurturing Healthy Relationships

The Foundation of a Fulfilling Life

In Chapter 25, Zohaib Hassan Khan explores the art of "Building and Nurturing Healthy Relationships," unraveling the key principles and habits that contribute to meaningful connections. This chapter delves into the dynamics of healthy relationships, offering insights and actionable steps to cultivate strong bonds in both personal and professional spheres.

**1. Foundations of Healthy Relationships:

Establishing Core Principles:* Khan sets the groundwork by defining the essential elements of healthy relationships.

Action Steps:

Reflect on your values and priorities in relationships.

Establish open communication as a cornerstone for building healthy connections.

**2. Effective Communication Skills:

Communication as a Relationship Pillar:* Khan guides readers in honing effective communication skills for stronger connections.

Action Steps:

Practice active listening and validate the perspectives of others.

Express thoughts and feelings clearly and empathetically.

**3. Empathy and Emotional Intelligence:

Understanding others:* Khan explores the role of empathy and emotional intelligence in fostering deeper connections.

Action Steps:

Cultivate self-awareness to better understand your own emotions.

Practice empathy by putting yourself in others' shoes and acknowledging their feelings.

**4. Building Trust and Reliability:

Trust as the Bedrock:* Khan emphasizes the importance of trust and reliability in relationship building.

Action Steps:

Demonstrate consistency and reliability in your actions.

Be transparent and honest to build and maintain trust.

**5. Resolving Conflicts Constructively:

Conflict as an Opportunity:* Khan guides readers in approaching conflicts as opportunities for growth in relationships.

Action Steps:

Develop conflict resolution skills, focusing on collaboration rather than confrontation.

Seek compromise and find common ground to resolve differences.

**6. Balancing Independence and Togetherness:

Harmony in Individuality:* Khan explores the delicate balance between maintaining individuality and fostering togetherness.

Action Steps:

Encourage personal growth and independence within the relationship.

Foster shared experiences to strengthen the bond between individuals.

**7. Quality Time and Shared Experiences:

Nurturing Connection:* Khan discusses the significance of quality time and shared experiences in relationship-building.

Action Steps:

Prioritize spending meaningful time together.

Engage in activities that create lasting memories and deepen the connection.

**8. Supporting Each Other's Goals:

Mutual Growth:* Khan emphasizes the role of support in facilitating the achievement of individual and shared goals.

Action Steps:

Discuss and align personal and professional goals.

Actively support each other's aspirations and celebrate achievements.

**9. Cultivating Forgiveness and Letting Go:

Embracing Healing:* Khan guides readers in the art of forgiveness and letting go for the well-being of relationships.

Action Steps:

Practice forgiveness as a way to release resentment and foster healing.

Communicate openly about feelings and concerns to address issues constructively.

**10. Sustaining Long-Term Connections:

Commitment to Growth:* Khan concludes the chapter by highlighting the commitment required for sustaining long-term relationships.

Action Steps:

Continuously invest time and effort in the relationship.

Adapt and grow together, embracing the changes that come with different life stages.

Key Takeaways: The Essence of Meaningful Connections:

Relationships as a Source of Fulfillment:* Khan underscores that healthy relationships form the foundation of a fulfilling and enriched life.

Action Steps:

Prioritize the cultivation of healthy relationship habits, recognizing that meaningful connections contribute significantly to personal happiness and overall well-being.

Chapter 26: THE ART OF RESILIENCE AND OVERCOMING ADVERSITY

Thriving in the Face of Challenges

In Chapter 26, Zohaib Hassan Khan explores "The Art of Resilience and Overcoming Adversity," offering profound insights into navigating challenges and bouncing back from setbacks. This chapter delves into the principles of resilience, providing actionable steps to cultivate a resilient mindset and thrive in the face of adversity.

**1. Understanding Resilience:

Foundational Principles:* Khan establishes the core principles of resilience and its transformative power.

Action Steps:

Embrace challenges as opportunities for growth and learning.

Cultivate a mindset that views setbacks as temporary and surmountable.

**2. Adapting to Change:

Flexibility as a Resilience Pillar:* Khan guides readers in embracing change as a key aspect of resilience.

Action Steps:

Develop adaptability by actively seeking new experiences.

View change as a natural part of life, fostering a positive and flexible mindset.

**3. Building Emotional Strength:

Emotional Intelligence in Resilience:* Khan explores the role of emotional strength in navigating adversity.

Action Steps:

Cultivate self-awareness to understand and manage your emotions.

Develop healthy coping mechanisms to navigate stress and challenges.

**4. Positive Thinking and Optimism:

Mindset Shift for Resilience:* Khan emphasizes the transformative power of positive thinking in building resilience.

Action Steps:

Challenge negative thoughts and cultivate a more optimistic outlook.

Focus on solutions rather than dwelling on problems during challenging times.

**5. Seeking Support and Connection:

Strength in Community:* Khan guides readers in leveraging social support as a crucial element of resilience.

Action Steps:

Reach out to friends, family, or a support network during challenging times.

Foster connections and build a community of support to navigate adversity.

**6. Learning from Setbacks:

Resilience through Reflection:* Khan explores the importance of learning from setbacks for personal growth.

Action Steps:

Reflect on challenges and setbacks to extract valuable lessons.

Use setbacks as opportunities to refine goals and strategies.

****7. Maintaining a Growth Mindset:**

Mindset Shift for Resilience:* Khan discusses the role of a growth mindset in fostering resilience.

Action Steps:

Embrace challenges as opportunities for learning and development.

Continuously seek to expand skills and knowledge, even in the face of adversity.

****8. Crisis Preparedness:**

Proactive Resilience:* Khan emphasizes the importance of preparedness in building resilience.

Action Steps:

Develop contingency plans for potential challenges.

Regularly assess and update crisis management strategies.

****9. Balancing Realism and Positivity:**

Optimism Grounded in Reality:* Khan guides readers in striking a balance between realism and positivity in resilience.

Action Steps:

Acknowledge challenges realistically without succumbing to pessimism.

Approach problems with a solution-oriented mindset, seeking positive outcomes.

**10. Teaching Resilience to Others:

Community Impact:* Khan concludes the chapter by highlighting the role of teaching and sharing resilience with others.

Action Steps:

Mentor and support others in developing their resilience.

Foster a culture of resilience in communities and organizations.

Key Takeaways: The Resilience Mindset for Thriving:

Resilience as a Lifelong Journey:* Khan underscores that resilience is not a destination but a continuous journey of growth and adaptation.

Action Steps:

Embrace challenges with resilience, recognizing them as opportunities for personal development.

Cultivate a mindset that not only withstands adversity but thrives and evolves through it.

Chapter 27: THE ENTREPRENEURIAL MINDSET

Igniting Innovation and Seizing Opportunities

In Chapter 27, Zohaib Hassan Khan explores "The Entrepreneurial Mindset," unveiling the key principles and habits that define the mindset of successful entrepreneurs. This chapter delves into the entrepreneurial spirit, providing insights and actionable steps to foster innovation, seize opportunities, and navigate the dynamic landscape of entrepreneurship.

**1. Defining the Entrepreneurial Mindset:

Core Characteristics:* Khan establishes the foundational characteristics that define an entrepreneurial mindset.

Action Steps:

Embrace a mindset of innovation and adaptability.

Cultivate a willingness to take calculated risks in pursuit of opportunities.

**2. Innovation and Creativity:

Driving Forces of Entrepreneurship:* Khan guides readers in harnessing the power of innovation and creativity.

Action Steps:

Foster a culture of creativity by encouraging new ideas and perspectives.

Actively seek out and explore innovative solutions to challenges.

**3. Risk-Taking and Calculated Gambles:

Strategic Risk Assessment:* Khan explores the art of taking calculated risks to propel entrepreneurial ventures.

Action Steps:

Assess risks systematically, weighing potential rewards against possible drawbacks.

Embrace a mindset that views failure as a valuable learning experience.

**4. Visionary Leadership:

Guiding the Entrepreneurial Journey:* Khan emphasizes the role of visionary leadership in entrepreneurial success.

Action Steps:

Develop a clear and compelling vision for your entrepreneurial venture.

Inspire and motivate others by effectively communicating your vision.

**5. Adaptability in a Dynamic Environment:

Navigating Change:* Khan guides readers in navigating the dynamic nature of entrepreneurial endeavors.

Action Steps:

Embrace change as an inherent part of entrepreneurship.

Develop the ability to pivot and adapt strategies based on evolving circumstances.

**6. Continuous Learning and Growth:

Lifelong Entrepreneurial Education:* Khan explores the importance of continual learning and personal growth.

Action Steps:

Stay abreast of industry trends and advancements through continuous education.

Cultivate a growth mindset that views challenges as opportunities for development.

**7. Networking and Relationship Building:

Collaborative Entrepreneurship:* Khan emphasizes the significance of networking and building meaningful relationships.

Action Steps:

Actively engage in networking events and communities within your industry.

Foster mutually beneficial relationships that contribute to the growth of your entrepreneurial venture.

**8. Customer-Centric Approach:

Understanding and Meeting Customer Needs:* Khan guides readers in adopting a customer-centric approach.

Action Steps:

Regularly gather feedback from customers to understand their needs and preferences.

Use customer insights to refine products or services and enhance the overall customer experience.

**9. Resilience in the Face of Setbacks:

Bouncing Back from Challenges:* Khan explores the role of resilience in entrepreneurial endeavors.

Action Steps:

Develop resilience by viewing setbacks as learning experiences.

Continuously reassess and refine strategies in response to challenges.

**10. Execution and Implementation Excellence:

Turning Ideas into Reality:* Khan concludes the chapter by highlighting the importance of effective execution.

Action Steps:

Focus on implementing ideas with precision and excellence.

Develop a strategic plan for executing business goals and objectives.

Key Takeaways: Cultivating the Entrepreneurial Spirit:

Entrepreneurship as a Mindset:* Khan underscores that entrepreneurship is not just a profession but a mindset that can be cultivated and embraced.

Action Steps:

Internalize the core characteristics of the entrepreneurial mindset, applying them to your endeavors and pursuits.

Approach challenges and opportunities with an entrepreneurial spirit, fostering innovation, adaptability, and a commitment to continuous growth.

Chapter 28: THE POWER OF GIVING BACK

Creating Impact through Generosity

In Chapter 28, Zohaib Hassan Khan explores "The Power of Giving Back," shedding light on the transformative impact of generosity and philanthropy. This chapter delves into the principles of giving back, offering insights and actionable steps to make a positive difference in the lives of others and contribute to the betterment of society.

**1. Understanding the Joy of Giving:

Intrinsic Rewards:* Khan establishes the profound joy and fulfillment that come from giving back.

Action Steps:

Reflect on personal values and identify causes that resonate with you.

Embrace a mindset of generosity, recognizing the impact of giving on both individuals and communities.

**2. Identifying Causes and Passions:

Personalizing Philanthropy:* Khan guides readers in identifying causes and passions that align with their values.

Action Steps:

Explore a variety of charitable causes to find those that resonate deeply.

Prioritize alignment with personal values to maximize the impact of giving.

**3. Time and Talent Contributions:

Beyond Financial Giving:* Khan explores the various ways individuals can contribute time and talents to make a difference.

Action Steps:

Identify skills and expertise that can be shared with organizations in need.

Allocate time regularly for volunteer work and community service.

**4. Strategic Philanthropy:

Maximizing Impact:* Khan emphasizes the importance of strategic thinking in philanthropy for meaningful impact.

Action Steps:

Research and select organizations that align with your values and have a proven track record of effectiveness.

Consider forming partnerships with like-minded individuals or organizations to amplify impact.

**5. Corporate Social Responsibility (CSR):

Businesses Making a Difference:* Khan explores the role of businesses in contributing to societal well-being through CSR.

Action Steps:

Integrate social responsibility into business practices and operations.

Engage employees in philanthropic initiatives to foster a culture of giving within the organization.

**6. Impactful Giving on a Budget:

Resourceful Philanthropy:* Khan provides insights into making a meaningful impact even with limited resources.

Action Steps:

Set a budget for philanthropic activities and stick to it.

Explore creative ways to contribute, such as organizing community events or fundraising campaigns.

**7. Engaging in Community Initiatives:

Local Contributions:* Khan emphasizes the impact of community-level initiatives in creating positive change.

Action Steps:

Get involved in local organizations and initiatives that address community needs.

Attend town hall meetings or community gatherings to understand specific challenges and opportunities.

**8. Educational Philanthropy:

Empowering Through Education:* Khan explores the transformative power of investing in education.

Action Steps:

Support educational programs and initiatives that provide access to quality education.

Consider establishing scholarships or mentorship programs to empower individuals through learning.

**9. Creating Sustainable Impact:

Long-Term Vision:* Khan guides readers in fostering sustainable impact through philanthropy.

Action Steps:

Collaborate with organizations that prioritize long-term, sustainable solutions.

Monitor and evaluate the impact of contributions over time, adjusting strategies as needed.

**10. Inspiring a Culture of Giving:

Catalyzing Collective Generosity:* Khan concludes the chapter by highlighting the importance of inspiring others to give back.

Action Steps:

Share personal philanthropic experiences to inspire others.

Encourage friends, family, and colleagues to join in giving back, creating a ripple effect of positive change.

Key Takeaways: The Ripple Effect of Generosity:

Generosity as a Catalyst:* Khan underscores that giving back has a transformative ripple effect, creating positive change for individuals and communities.

Action Steps:

Embrace the joy of giving and recognize the power of even small contributions to make a meaningful impact.

Cultivate a culture of generosity in personal and professional spheres, contributing to a more compassionate and connected world.

Chapter 29: EMBRACING LIFELONG LEARNING

Unlocking Personal and Professional Growth

In Chapter 29, Zohaib Hassan Khan explores the theme of "Embracing Lifelong Learning," highlighting the significance of continuous education for personal and professional development. This chapter delves into the principles of lifelong learning, offering insights and actionable steps to foster a commitment to acquiring knowledge and skills throughout life.

1. The Power of Continuous Growth:

Lifelong Learning as a Catalyst:* Khan establishes the transformative power of continuous growth through learning.

Action Steps:

Recognize the value of lifelong learning in staying relevant and adaptable.

Embrace a mindset that views learning as a lifelong journey rather than a finite destination.

2. Cultivating a Growth Mindset:

Mindset Shift for Lifelong Learning:* Khan guides readers in adopting a growth mindset that fuels continuous learning.

Action Steps:

Embrace challenges as opportunities for learning and improvement.

View failures as stepping stones toward growth and mastery.

**3. Formal and Informal Learning Channels:

Diverse Learning Opportunities:* Khan explores a variety of formal and informal channels for lifelong learning.

Action Steps:

Enroll in courses, workshops, or certifications relevant to personal and professional goals.

Leverage informal learning through reading, podcasts, and online resources.

**4. Building a Personal Learning Plan:

Strategic Learning Approach:* Khan emphasizes the importance of developing a personalized learning plan.

Action Steps:

Identify specific learning goals and objectives.

Create a structured plan outlining the steps and resources needed to achieve these goals.

**5. Networking for Learning Opportunities:

Learning through Collaboration:* Khan guides readers in leveraging networking for expanded learning opportunities.

Action Steps:

Attend industry events, conferences, and seminars to connect with experts and peers.

Join professional networks and online communities to access valuable insights and knowledge.

**6. Adopting Technology for Learning:

Tech-Driven Educational Tools:* Khan explores the role of technology in facilitating lifelong learning.

Action Steps:

Utilize online platforms, apps, and educational tools to enhance learning experiences.

Stay informed about emerging technologies that can support continuous education.

**7. Cross-Disciplinary Learning:

Holistic Knowledge Integration:* Khan emphasizes the benefits of exploring diverse disciplines for holistic learning.

Action Steps:

Venture into areas outside your core expertise to gain interdisciplinary insights.

Seek connections between different fields to foster creativity and innovation.

**8. Mentorship and Learning from Others:

Guidance for Growth:* Khan explores the role of mentorship in facilitating continuous learning.

Action Steps:

Seek out mentors who can provide guidance and share their experiences.

Actively listen and learn from the experiences of others in your professional or personal network.

**9. Reflection and Application:

Integrating Learning into Life:* Khan guides readers in the importance of reflection and practical application of knowledge.

Action Steps:

Reflect on learning experiences and consider how new knowledge can be applied in real-life scenarios.

Create opportunities to practice and reinforce newly acquired skills.

**10. Fostering a Learning Culture:

Encouraging Continuous Education:* Khan concludes the chapter by highlighting the importance of fostering a culture of continuous learning.

Action Steps:

Encourage a learning mindset within organizations, communities, and families.

Share your learning journey with others, inspiring them to embark on their path of lifelong learning.

Key Takeaways: The Journey of Lifelong Learning:

Learning as a Lifestyle:* Khan underscores that lifelong learning is not a destination but a continuous journey of growth and development.

Action Steps:

Embrace the joy of learning and recognize the limitless possibilities for personal and professional enrichment.

Cultivate a commitment to continuous education, fostering a mindset that seeks knowledge, embraces challenges, and thrives on the journey of lifelong learning.

Chapter 30: LEGACY BUILDING AND LEAVING A LASTING IMPACT

Crafting a Meaningful and Enduring Contribution

In the final chapter of "30 Habits of Millionaires That You Should Have," Zohaib Hassan Khan explores the theme of "Legacy Building and Leaving a Lasting Impact." This chapter delves into the principles of creating a meaningful legacy that transcends personal success and contributes positively to the world. Khan provides insights and actionable steps to guide readers in crafting a legacy that endures beyond their lifetime.

1. Defining Your Legacy:

Clarifying Values and Impact:* Khan establishes the importance of defining one's legacy based on personal values and desired impact.

Action Steps:

Reflect on the values that matter most to you.

Identify the positive impact you want to make in your community, industry, or the world.

2. Aligning Actions with Values:

Living a Legacy-Driven Life:* Khan guides readers in aligning daily actions with the values that define their legacy.

Action Steps:

Evaluate current actions and behaviors in light of your desired legacy.

Make intentional choices that reflect your values and contribute to your envisioned impact.

**3. Community and Social Contribution:

Building Bridges and Making a Difference:* Khan explores the role of community and social contribution in legacy building.

Action Steps:

Identify ways to give back to your community and address social issues.

Establish or participate in initiatives that contribute to positive change on a broader scale.

**4. Investing in Future Generations:

Educational and Mentorship Initiatives:* Khan emphasizes the impact of investing in the development of future generations.

Action Steps:

Support educational programs and initiatives that empower young individuals.

Mentor and guide aspiring individuals to help them navigate their paths to success.

**5. Environmental Stewardship:

Sustainable Practices for a Better World:* Khan discusses the importance of environmental stewardship in leaving a positive impact.

Action Steps:

Adopt sustainable practices in personal and professional life.

Support or engage in initiatives focused on environmental conservation and awareness.

**6. Philanthropic Endeavors:

Creating Lasting Change:* Khan explores the transformative power of philanthropy in building a lasting legacy.

Action Steps:

Identify causes or organizations aligned with your values for philanthropic support.

Establish or contribute to initiatives that address systemic issues and create sustainable change.

**7. Documenting and Sharing Your Wisdom:

Legacy through Knowledge:* Khan guides readers in documenting and sharing their wisdom for the benefit of others.

Action Steps:

Record personal experiences, insights, and lessons learned.

Share knowledge through writing, speaking engagements, or mentorship programs.

**8. Family and Personal Relationships:

Nurturing Lasting Connections:* Khan emphasizes the role of family and personal relationships in legacy building.

Action Steps:

Prioritize quality time and meaningful interactions with family and loved ones.

Contribute to the well-being and success of those closest to you.

**9. Innovative Contributions to Society:

Pioneering Impactful Solutions:* Khan explores the impact of innovative contributions in leaving a lasting mark.

Action Steps:

Identify opportunities for innovation within your field or community.

Contribute to the development of solutions that address pressing challenges.

**10. Reflection and Evaluation:

Continual Refinement of Legacy:* Khan concludes the chapter by highlighting the importance of reflection and evaluation in refining one's legacy.

Action Steps:

Regularly assess the alignment of actions with values and impact.

Adjust and refine the components of your legacy to ensure continued relevance and positive influence.

Key Takeaways: Crafting a Legacy of Significance:

Legacy as a Purposeful Contribution:* Khan underscores that a meaningful legacy is crafted through intentional actions and contributions.

Action Steps:

Embrace the responsibility of leaving a positive impact beyond personal success.

Continuously refine and expand your legacy, recognizing that the journey of legacy building is a lifelong commitment to creating a lasting and meaningful contribution to the world.

Conclusion:

In "30 Habits of Millionaires That You Should Have," Zohaib Hassan Khan has masterfully woven a tapestry of wisdom, guiding readers on a transformative journey towards personal and financial success. Through a meticulous exploration of habits, Khan not only shares insights into the habits of millionaires but provides actionable steps for readers to incorporate these habits into their own lives.

Zohaib Hassan Khan, a visionary author, brings a unique blend of experience and expertise to the realm of personal development and financial success. His commitment to empowering individuals shines through each chapter, offering a roadmap for those who aspire to achieve greatness.

As readers embark on this enriching journey, they are not only equipped with practical strategies for financial prosperity but also inspired to cultivate a mindset of continuous growth, resilience, and generosity. Beyond the pursuit of wealth, Khan emphasizes the importance of leaving a lasting legacy—one that extends beyond personal success and positively impacts communities and future generations.

In the words of Zohaib Hassan Khan:

"Success is not just measured by the wealth we accumulate but by the positive impact we create in the lives of others. Your legacy is not defined by what you have but by the meaningful contributions you make."

This poignant quote encapsulates the essence of Khan's philosophy—a philosophy that transcends monetary success and underscores the profound significance of contributing to the well-being of others and leaving a legacy of lasting impact.

As readers reflect on the invaluable lessons imparted by Zohaib Hassan Khan, they are not merely recipients of knowledge but torchbearers of a transformative legacy—one that embraces lifelong learning, resilience, and the power of giving back. The journey doesn't end with the last page but extends into the reader's commitment to applying these principles and habits for a richer, more purposeful life.

Zohaib Hassan Khan's work stands as a testament to the belief that true success is a holistic endeavor—one that encompasses financial prosperity, personal growth, and a legacy of positive influence. In the spirit of his teachings, readers are encouraged to go forth, embrace the habits of millionaires, and carve a path of success that radiates far beyond individual achievement.